More
PAPER SCULPTURE
A STEP-BY-STEP GUIDE

edited by

KATHLEEN ZIEGLER

and

NICK GRECO

Dimensional Illustrators, Inc.
Southampton, Pennsylvania USA

HBI
Hearst Books International
New York, NY USA

First Published by

Dimensional Illustrators, Inc.
For Hearst Books International
1350 Avenue of the Americas
New York, NY 10019 USA

Distributed in the USA and Canada by

North Light Books,
an imprint of F&W Publications
1507 Dana Avenue
Cincinnati, OH 45207 USA
ISBN 0-688-15379-8

Distributed throughout the rest of the world by

Hearst Books International
1350 Avenue of the Americas
New York, NY 10019 USA
Fax: 212-261-6795
ISBN 0-688-15379-8

First published in Singapore by

Page One Publishing Pte Ltd
Block 4 Pasir Panjang Road
#08-37 Alexandra Distripark
Singapore 118491
65-2743188 *Telephone*
65-2741833 *Fax*
ISBN 981-00-8932-5

Address direct mail and electronic sales to

Dimensional Illustrators, Inc.
362 2nd Street Pike/Suite 112
Southampton, PA 18966 USA
215.953.1415 *Telephone*
215.953.1697 *Fax*
dimension@3DimIllus.com *Email*
http://www.3DimIllus.com *Website*

More Paper Sculpture: A Step-By-Step Guide
Kathleen Ziegler, Nick Greco

Printed in Singapore

CREDITS

Creative Director/Associate Editor
Kathleen Ziegler
Dimensional Illustrators, Inc.

Executive Editor
Nick Greco
Dimensional Illustrators, Inc.

Book, Cover Design & Typography
Melissa Walter
MWdesign/Bensalem, PA
215-639-4181

Step-By-Step Photography
Kathleen Ziegler
pp.38-43
Yoshihiro Ishii

Copywriter
Rachael Allendar

Hand Model
Jennifer Walter

Copy Consultant
Leona Mangol

Paper Sculpture Cover
Carol Jeanotilla
©1997 Copyright Carol Jeanotilla.
All Rights Reserved.

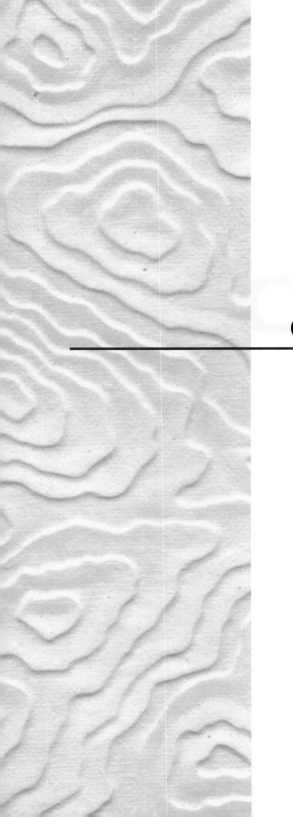

Contents

INTRODUCTION

Immerse yourself in the pristine world of paper sculpture. This book is for anyone who enjoys creating with their hands and wants to explore the dynamic and distinctive power this unique material offers. Artists who work with this medium are drawn to the beauty and simplicity of its basic elements. Made from the natural fibers of cotton and wood pulp, paper has the tensile strength combined with the supple flexibility for delicate manip- 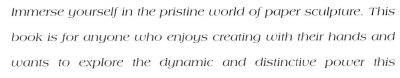 *ulation. It is a material so common and familiar that it can easily be overlooked, but within creative hands, a universe of possibilities unfolds.*

Throughout the centuries, cultures from around the world have tapped this potential, creating intricately detailed sculptural images. As early as the 1920s, paper sculpture was used as a commercial medium in the United States. Initially, the work was designed for store window displays. The advent

of photography in print lead to the inclusion of paper illustrations of products in newspaper and magazine advertisements. Innovative art directors and artists quickly realized that the symbolic imagery used in store windows could bring eye-catching power and appeal to the print medium. This advertisement from 1932 portrayed the pristine quality of Ivory soap as a paper illustration. Using clean white materials and inventive nuance, the ad combines a charming story with lively, graceful design to represent the product.

From its inception, paper sculpture has captured the

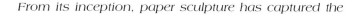

viewer's imagination. Its popularity has continued and artists have never ceased to explore its wonderful possibilities. **More Paper Sculpture** *showcases the best work of ten, award winners of the 3Dimensional Art Directors and Illustrators Awards Show from the United States, Mexico, Brazil and Japan. Founded in 1989, the competition is an international exhibition which recognizes and honors excellence in 3D illustration. Each year Gold, Silver and Bronze awards are presented to artists for their ingenious dimensional creations. Paper illustrations consistently appear in advertisements, editorials, books, posters, greeting* cards, as well as, galleries and private commissions. Paper sculptors have proven to be an essential part of the illustration and fine arts industry. This book offers a glimpse into this energetic and exciting creative arena.

More Paper Sculpture: A Step-By-Step Guide presents the vision and dynamic strategies of the most accomplished paper sculptors. Novice and expert alike can share in the discoveries and insights offered in this remarkable publication. Each artist demonstrates the creative process of one featured paper sculpture project in simple, easy-to-follow steps, detailing basic techniques and methods. Four separate chapters explore the magic of these talented visionaries. While each sculptor has developed a distinct personal style, certain shared attributes

allow for the book to be divided into White, Pigmented, Embellished and Specialty Papers. A full-color gallery of work completes the chapter showcasing each artist's portfolio.

Full of insights and dazzling surprises, the projects featured in this book will ignite your imagination. Every artist has let their interest lead them into original experimentation. **More Paper Sculpture** invites readers to join in this exciting journey through the enchanting world of this extraordinary art. With ordinary tools and conventional sheets of paper anyone can discover its magic. We hope the illustrations and ideas presented will inspire you to pursue your own vision with this fascinating medium.

-Kathleen Ziegler and Nick Greco

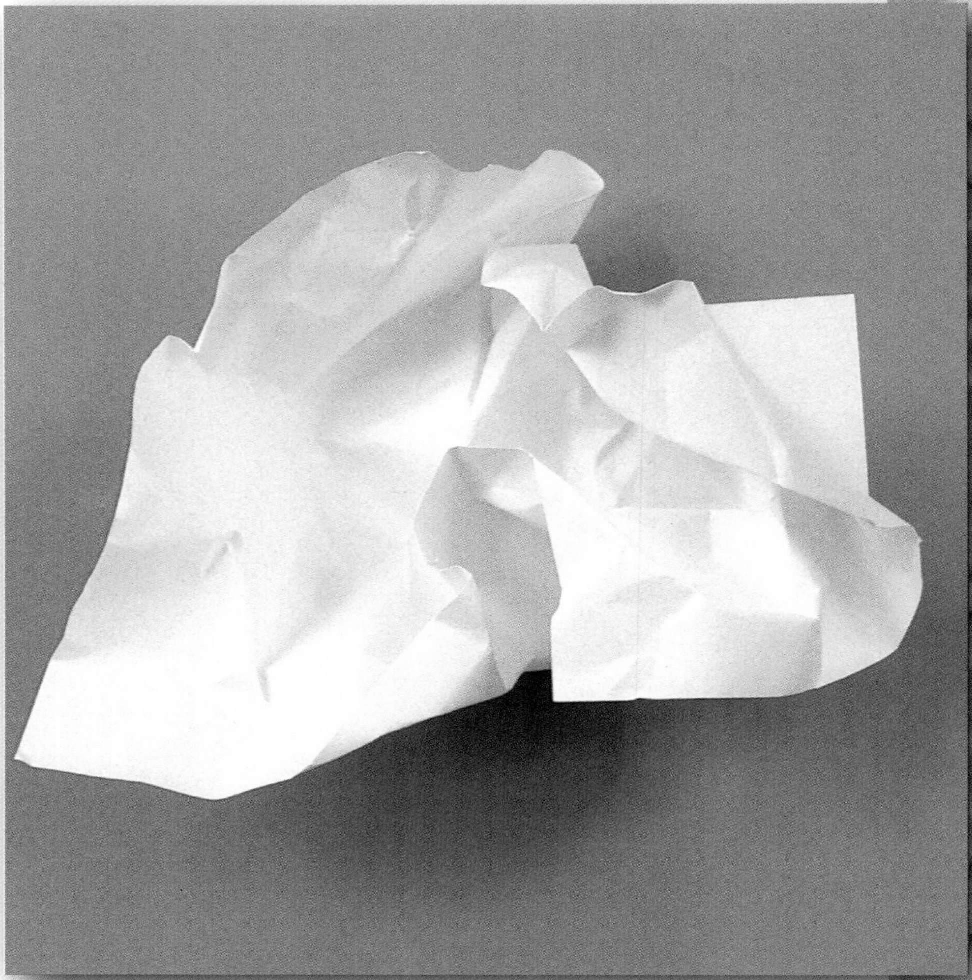

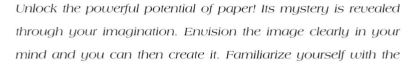

CREATIVITY

Unlock the powerful potential of paper! Its mystery is revealed through your imagination. Envision the image clearly in your mind and you can then create it. Familiarize yourself with the nature of paper through inventive exploration. Flexible yet strong, a sheet of paper can be folded, scored, curled and shaped without tearing. Commercial papers will react differently than handmade papers. Your ideas will determine the most appropriate ones to use for your project. Each artist in this book uses distinct papers that reflect their personal design process. By practicing with sample papers, you will achieve your own style and appreciation for this extraordinary artform.

This delicate material is comprised of a network of interlocking natural fibers. Implement the scoring and curling methods on a variety of papers. Apply the techniques several times on small samples. Create a miniature-size version of your project on plain, inexpensive paper and work out the basic pieces first. Then, create another small model of the design, using the selected papers. Through consistent practice and exercise, you will attain the skills needed to turn your ideas into exceptional dimensional designs of light and shadow!

13

Commercial and handmade papers offer an unlimited palette from which to create. Machine-formed sheets have a greater flexibility in the direction of the fibers or grain. Canson, Strathmore and Bristol papers are excellent primary choices. They are available in a wide array of weights and bright colors. Hot press (smooth surface) and cold press (rough surface) afford elegant textural variations.

Handmade papers are imbedded with fascinating fibers ranging from delicate tissue-thin lace, to more textural weights. Easily manipulated, they can be shaped in any direction because of the random grain pattern. Acid-free papers are paramount for ensuring the longevity of the sculpture. Hand formed sheets encompass Eastern, Western, watercolor and printmaking papers.

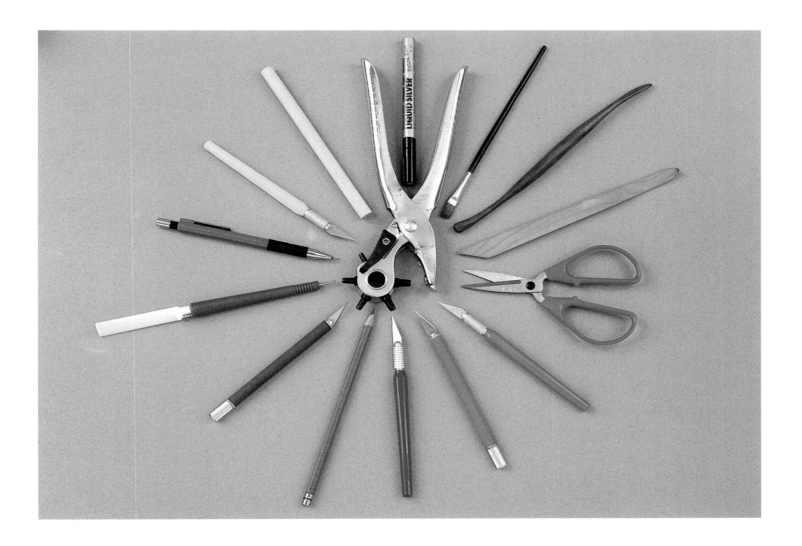

A color wheel of common tools can be utilized to create paper sculpture. In conjunction with a standard art knife, many everyday materials will enable you to begin designing with paper. A wooden clay tool, a dental pick, and even a leather punch with a rotating head can be implemented to perform various techniques. Through continued experimentation, household gadgets, in conjunction with artists tools, offer unlimited possibilities. And, with a little ingenuity and inspiration, a flat piece of paper can be transformed into an intricate design of depth and dimension.

15

Basics

It will gently conform to any shape when manipulated. Crush a piece of paper in your hand and lightly flatten it out. Notice how the creases capture a nuance of shadows. This enchanting characteristic is the magic that makes paper a special medium. Paper sculptures are designed to gather light and shadow to create an illusion of depth.

Grain

When machine-made papers are formed, the fibers are aligned in one direction. This is called the grain. Paper will curl and fold easily in the direction of the grain. To determine the grain, cut two sample pieces of paper and fold them perpendicular to each other. The piece with the smoothest crease determines the optimum direction for curling and folding.

White Paper

The pristine quality of white paper is most evident when used in its purist form. Through the contrast of hot and cold press papers, variances of light and shadow are most evident. Although it has a graceful fresh appeal, artists must guard against soiling the paper during construction. Maintaining cleanliness is essential for the integrity of a white paper sculpture.

Embellished Paper

Any color enhancement should be tested on a sample first. Spattering and sponging give a random, overall pattern. Spray painting provides gradations of tones and shades while water colors add a flowing tint to the surface. Colored pencils add bold strokes of pigment to the paper. An abundance of embellishments are available to enhance the paper surface.

Pigmented Paper

Canson construction, Fabriano, Strathmore, Color-aid and assorted pigmented papers provide an array of colors. Laser paper is also available in a variety of tonal blends. Rich hues and a gradation of delicate shades offer a limitless spectrum to the paper palette.

17

Specialty Paper

Handmade papers are a specialty. Western papers are extremely thin and have a very firm tensile strength. Eastern papers are full of textural fibers and are easy to form. Rice papers add a delicate, airy grace while the opacity of marbled papers renders swirls of intense color. Surface texture and density are affected by the use of these particular sheets.

Cutting

There are many knife blade shapes and sizes, but the #11 is the best for cutting paper. New rubber-grip handles offer the artist precise handling and versatility. Free-form shapes are produced effortlessly using small scissors. The rotating knife blade tip provides excellent traction for cutting curves, and the compass blade cutter is ideal for making circles. Blades must be changed often to keep a sharp, exact cutting edge.

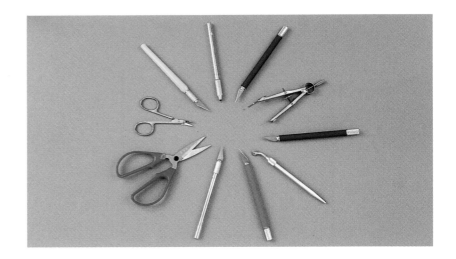

Cutting Mats

A proper cutting mat is crucial to ensure a clean precise cut. Self-healing plastic mats are excellent slicing surfaces. Using cardboard or foamcore as a cutting surface results in a dull blade and an unevenly trimmed edge as the cardboard erodes.

Adhesives

An assortment of adhesives is available for use with paper. White glue is the most popular because of its clear, quick-drying time. Hot glue guns are best for affixing heavier constructions. Foamtape adds dimension to a sculpture when building layers, and adhesive tape allows for non-permanent repositioning.

Embellishments

Numerous wet and dry media are suitable for use with paper to create dimensional effects. Watercolors produce a loose fluid approach when brushed or spattered. Airbrushed or spray paint presents an even tonal range of color values, while colored pencil and pastels yield added shadow and shade.

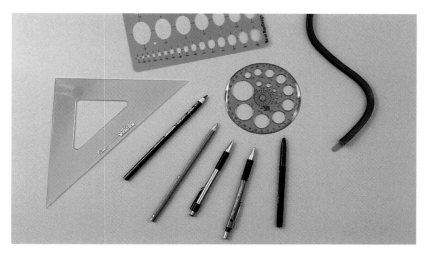

Drawing Tools

Drawing aids help facilitate the imaging process. HB pencils are excellent for loose concept sketches. For initial design layout, the flexible curve provides an adaptable edge to refine lines. Templates and triangles furnish precise patterns for final drawings.

19

Forming Tools

An assemblage of tools can be utilized to form and shape the paper. Compound curves are possible with round clay tools and metal burnishers. Wooden or plastic dowels provide ease in curling. Embossing is achieved through the use of knitting needles, burnishers and even dental tools.

1 Curling is the technique that gives the paper volume and dimension by rolling it around a given shape. First, find the direction of the grain. Then, draw a vertical line one inch from the edge of a piece of paper. Using a #11 art knife blade, cut out the thin strip.

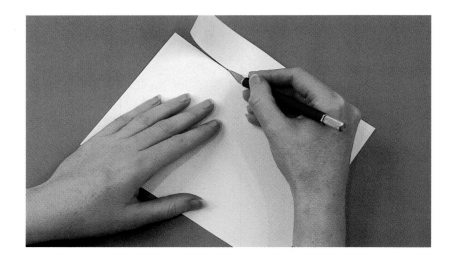

20

2 With one hand, hold the tip of the paper in place. Tightly wrap the strip all the way around a half inch wooden dowel and hold for five seconds. The paper should be rolled tighter than needed as it has a tendency to spring back slightly.

3 Release the paper slowly. A tighter curl can be achieved by using a smaller diameter dowel. The curl can be made larger by flexing the opening of the shape. The resiliency of the paper allows it to be re-curled as often as necessary.

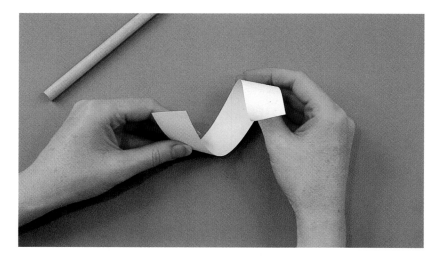

1 Scoring is the technique of cutting halfway through the paper thickness to provide a precise edge for folding the paper. Find the direction of the grain and draw a vertical line two inches from the edge of a piece of paper. Using a #11 art knife blade, cut the wide strip out completely.

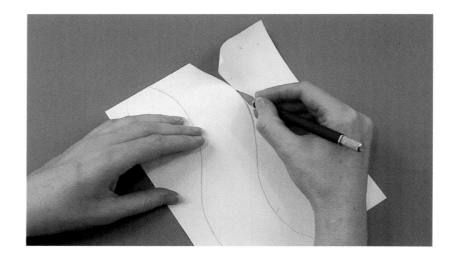

2 Draw another pencil line down the center of the strip. Pull the sharp art knife blade along the center line, cutting halfway through the thickness of the paper. Guide the knife with an even, smooth slice across the surface. The thickness of the paper will determine the exact pressure needed to create a perfectly scored line. These techniques require practice, patience and a gentle hand.

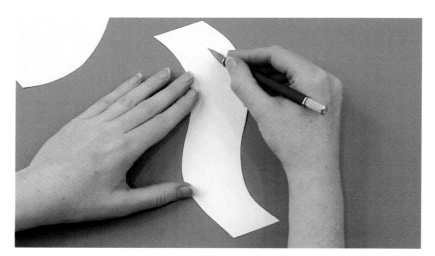

3 Fold the paper away from the line to create a smooth, precise bend. Alternating score cuts on the front and back of the paper will result in concave and convex folds. This technique adds dimension to the paper by creating flat angular planes which catch light and shadow.

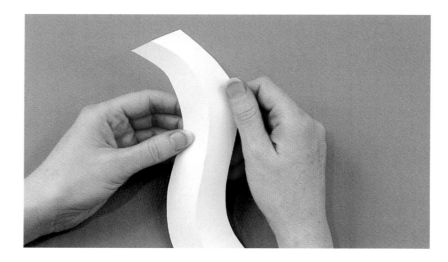

23

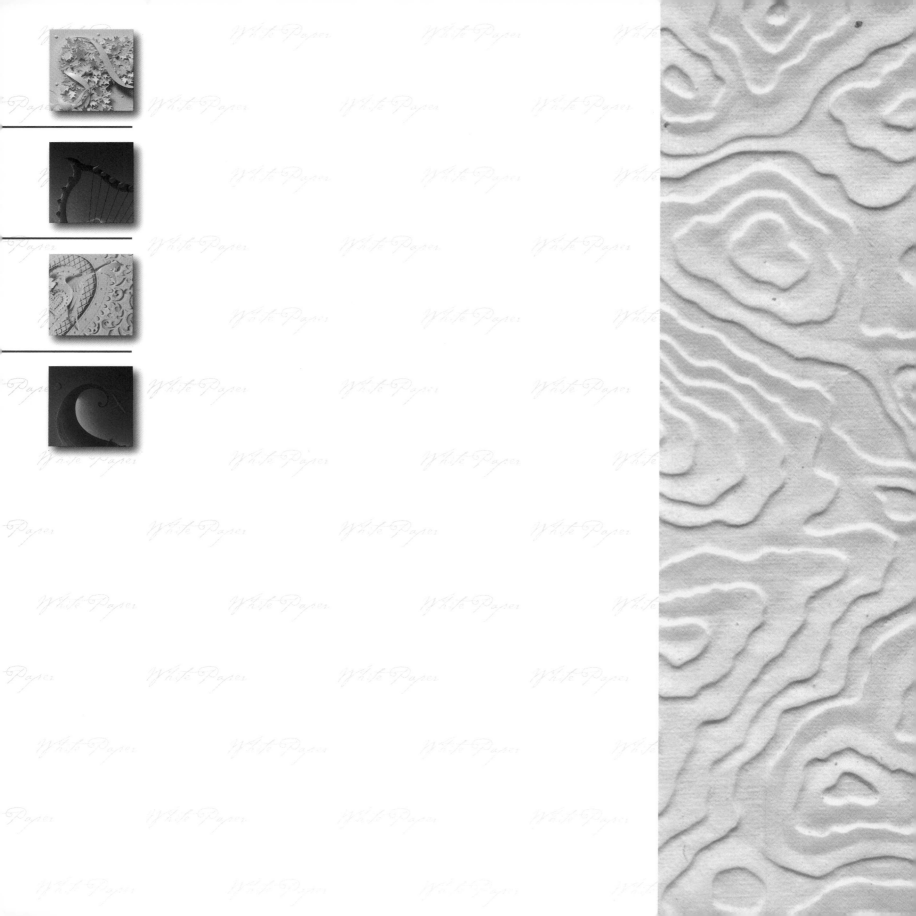

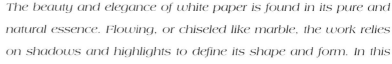

The beauty and elegance of white paper is found in its pure and natural essence. Flowing, or chiseled like marble, the work relies on shadows and highlights to define its shape and form. In this

WHITE PAPER

pristine medium, compound curves and subtle textures breathe life into the most basic material to create lively and meticulous visions. For the featured artists, the lack of color is not a hindrance. With limitless possibilities, each nuance and detail adds to the visual effect.

Johnna Bandle and Koji Nakamura bring a distinct and dynamic approach to white paper. Both are self-taught and have developed their signature style out of a personal love for paper sculpture. Nakamura's aesthetic acumen is inventive and dreamlike. His creations are delicate yet graceful. His work gives the illusion of depth while preserving clean flat planes, suggesting a storybook magic. Bandle's work has a fully dimensional appearance. She transforms the rich complexity of the natural world into elaborate and sophisticated sculptures. With an awareness for detail and a clear and exacting sensibility, her work provides a benchmark of excellence. Each artist utilizes the flexibility of the fibers and the power of imagination to appeal to the viewer.

25

JOHNNA BANDLE

Johnna Bandle has been producing paper sculptures for more than 15 years. She has an affinity for paper and enjoys the challenge of creating in the third dimension. A white paper purist at heart, Bandle's images have a pristine elegance which capture and hold the imagination of the viewer. Acid-free materials are preferred for their longevity and resistance to fading; To further enhance the effect, Johnna occasionally applies water-based paint with an airbrush. She photographs each model with soft-edged shadows, and often experiments with different lighting to achieve greater depth.

Bandle has received numerous accolades for her visually appealing creations, including Gold, Silver and Bronze awards from the 3Dimensional Art Directors and Illustrators Awards Show. Johnna's sculptures are produced primarily for the advertising market and she is recognized as one of the leading professionals in the industry. Clients include many of the top Fortune 500 companies. She enjoys working with paper and likes to dazzle viewers with her spectacular creations. Johnna is drawn to white paper because it has, "a classical style all its own."

1 An initial sketch of the scene is drawn in pencil on tracing paper. The design includes a white mat frame that surrounds the image. An opening for the mat is carefully measured for the background paper and full-scale pieces are positioned within the composition.

28

2 Each layer is traced from the initial sketch. All the components are redrawn separately on a larger piece of tracing paper to the outline drawing. The template is used as a guide to delineate accurately the exact form of the moon and curved forms. The perimeter of the shapes are drawn slightly bigger to allow for the curl of the paper.

3 Smooth white papers are selected and tested for flexibility and thickness. Paper that is too thick will not curl well. However, very thin paper is too translucent and will reveal supports within the sculpture. Pantone Color Simulator is used to choose the blue background. The sample chips allow for an exact match for custom commissions and for coordinating colors for wallpaper, rooms or offices.

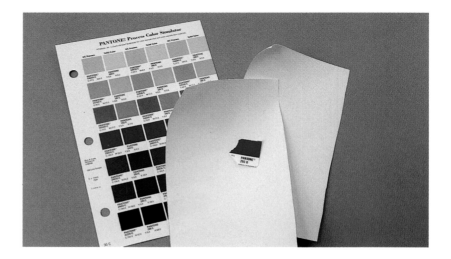

Johnna Bandle

The larger outline sketch is positioned face down on the lightbox. Using a sharp pencil, each element is transferred from the tracing paper to the back of the white paper. Careful attention is made to allow adequate space for cutting between every shape.

4

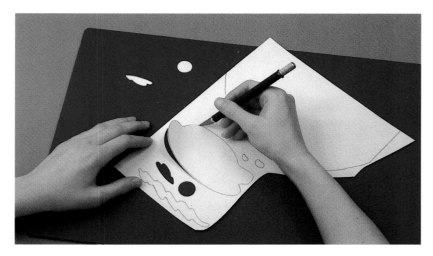

A #11 knife blade is used to cut out the patterns. Using a plastic cutting mat, the moon and clouds are gently cut from the backside of the select white paper. The blade is replaced often to ensure a clean precise edge. One smooth, continuous slice is made while turning the paper with the hand and guiding the knife along the pencil line.

5

The trees are made from several layers of paper. Many pieces are cut out for the large tree shape. At least fifteen separate elements are required for the overall form. The initial design layout is an important step in planning, to account for every cut piece of paper.

6

7 Once all the shapes are made, they are assembled according to size. A clean scrap of foamcore board is positioned on the cutting mat. Using a circular motion, a burnisher is used to press the underside of the tree edges into the foamcore. A smaller tool is used for the little edges toward the top of the tree. This creates a rolled effect, adding more dimension to the sculpture.

8 White acid-free glue is used to adhere the tree sections together. A thin line of glue is placed along the top edge of the tree part. The smaller piece is then positioned on the larger one. Each layer is designed to overlap slightly. Careful attention is made so that the adhesive does not seep onto the front surface of the paper. Working from the larger base, each layer is fastened in sequential order.

9 After the glue has dried on the assembled trees, they are curved into shape. The large tree is formed by gently bending the completed piece between the forefingers and thumbs. This technique should be done slowly to prevent the joined parts from cracking. The effect of the snow covered tree is achieved from the rolled edges and curved shaping.

Johnna Bandle

The blue background is achieved by airbrushing the matched color. It is then spray mounted to the white foamcore base. Foamcore spacers are used to create depth. The large curved foreground is positioned on top with adhesive foam tape. The tape is also attached to the front surface.

10

The large tree is positioned in place. A discreet pencil mark is used to indicate the exact spot. The backing from the foam tape is removed and the tree is attached in place. Once the pieces are adhered, it is very difficult to reposition them without tearing the sculpture.

11

31

Foam tape is placed on the underside of the moon, clouds and trees. Two smaller trees are delicately positioned in place and marked. The tape backing is removed and they are then permanently affixed. The moon is attached to the clouds and fastened to the background sky.

12

1 | Notecards On Lace Illustration

2 | Four Hearts Wrapping Paper

3 | Hearts With Doves Greeting Card

Johnna Bandle

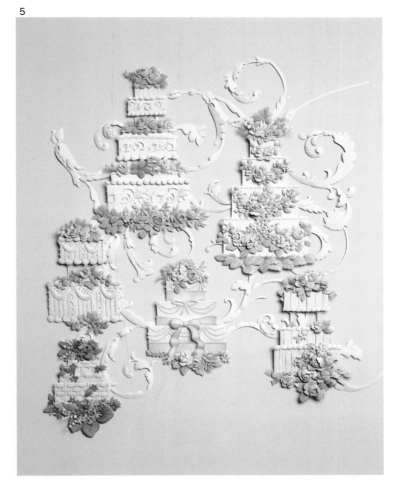

33

4 | *Wedding Cake Greeting Card*

5 | *Wedding Cake Illustration*

6 | *Sprint Holiday Card Postcard*

8

7

34

9

Johnna Bandle

35

Johnna Bandle

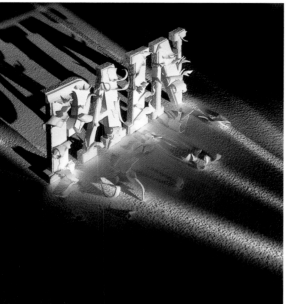

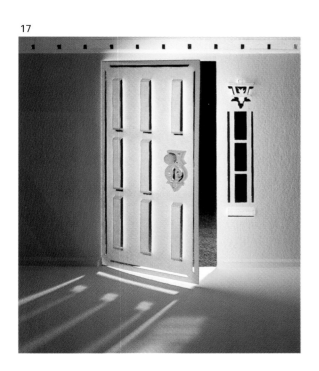

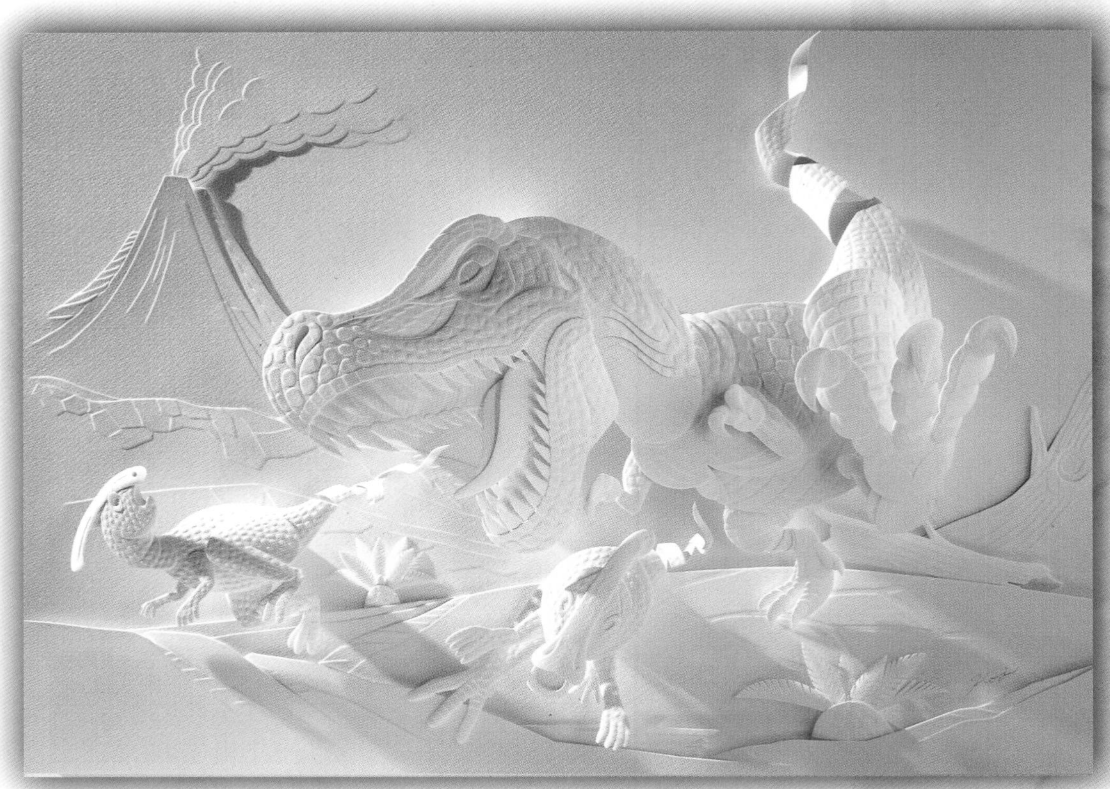

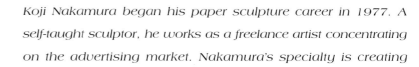

Koji Nakamura began his paper sculpture career in 1977. A self-taught sculptor, he works as a freelance artist concentrating on the advertising market. Nakamura's specialty is creating

KOJI NAKAMURA

images from white mermaid paper. This unique medium has the feel of human skin and adds a unique dimension to his work. The final design portrays an illustration that appears to be painted with light. He adds a significant amount of surface detail to the piece by pushing the paper through templates to produce a textured effect. Light and shadow are used to enhance the overall illusion of the sculpture.

His work has been recognized by the 3Dimensional Art Directors and Illustrators Awards Show. In 1991, Nakamura held a one-man exhibition in the Gallery House Maya, in Tokyo, Japan, and he is also the recipient of a Gold award at the New Year's Card Competition, held by the Shikoku Postal Service. With his unique style and attention to detail, Koji Nakamura is one of Japan's most respected and highly talented paper sculptors.

1 The concept of a dinosaur theme is designed on paper. A loose sketch is drawn that includes a Tyrannosaurus, with smaller dinosaurs and a volcano. The composition is refined and laid out to allow very precise areas of lighting when photographed.

2 Mermaid paper is selected because its surface feels like skin. The sketch is transferred onto a sheet of Kent paper, a thick sturdy material. The outline is made slightly larger to allow for the curve of the paper.

3 The base level forms are cut with a very sharp knife. The thick paper will act as a template for the elements. A smooth, continuous slicing motion is employed when cutting the paper.

K o j i   N a k a m u r a

A method for fabricating the skin surface texture is implemented. Numerous small openings are cut out of the Kent paper base elements. One skin pattern is made for each part of the dinosaur section.

4

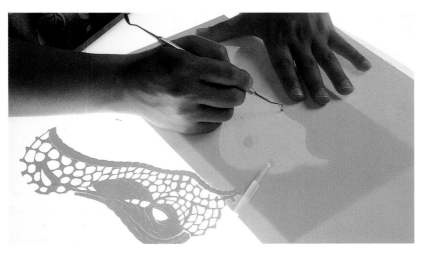

Using the cut-out opening from the previous step, the perimeter of the paper is embossed. The Mermaid paper is placed over the opening. Using a metal or glass tool with a rounded tip, the paper is gently and evenly pressed along the edge. This curved contour edge creates a natural effect to the artwork.

5

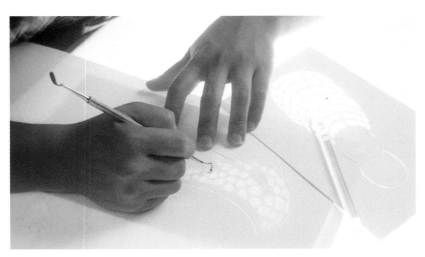

To create the scaly dinosaur skin texture, the pattern is turned over and positioned on a light box. The Mermaid paper is placed on top. With a delicate motion, the sheet is pushed into the small openings on the pattern with a metal tool. These shapes reflect the overall rough texture of the dinosaur skin.

6

After the sections have been embossed, they are curled and wooden dowels of various sizes are collected. Using a hand as a cushion, a large diameter dowel is rolled into the main body section of the Tyrannosaurus, forming a soft curl. Narrower diameters are used in the small areas for a tighter curl.

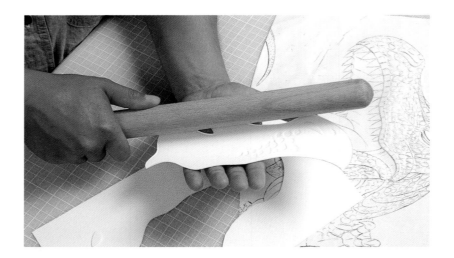

The finished curled sections are positioned in order and the main parts are glued to the large base. Spacers of double thick board are located periodically in levels to achieve dimension and shadow.

Two small dinosaur babies are cut from the original sketch. The skin is then formed pushing the paper through open pattern. They are curled using very narrow dowels. Using white glue, the parts are assembled with toothpicks.

Koji Nakamura

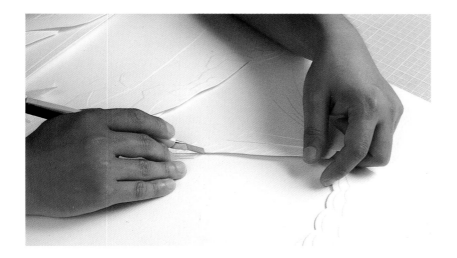

The background volcanic shapes are cut from a single sheet. The pieces are cut out around most of the edge, but not completely. By pressing the Mermaid paper into the overlay pattern, the edges are embossed. Care is taken to prevent the paper from getting dirty or creased.

10

All the assembled dinosaur parts are adhered together. Next, they are positioned on various angles, to enhance the foreshortened perspective. This effect adds drama and excitement to the scene.

43

11

The completed assemblage of dinosaurs is placed over the original sketch to check for balance and accuracy. The entire construction is attached to the volcanic scene. Adjustments are made to the shapes to refine the composition.

12

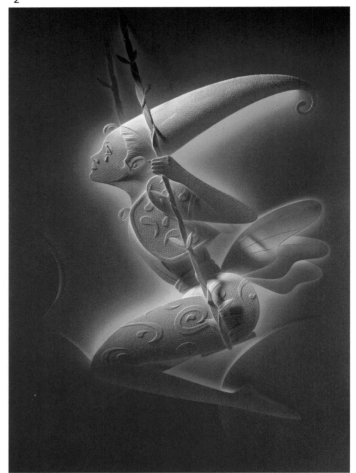

1 | Fall In Corso Poster

2 | Swinging Fairy Unpublished

3 | Fairy With Trumpet Self Promotion

Koji Nakamura

4 | *Water Fairy Self Promotion*

5 | *Dinosaur Self Promotion*

6 | *Humpback Whale Self Promotion*

7

9

8

10

7	Billie Holiday Jazz Series
8	Ella Fitzgerald Jazz Series
9	Michael Brecker Jazz Series
10	Keith Jarrett Jazz Series

Koji Nakamura

11

13

47

12

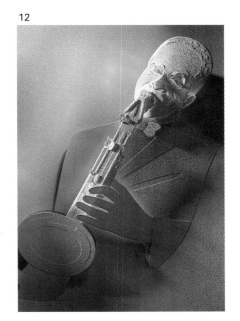

14

11	Count Basie Jazz Series
12	John Coltrane Jazz Series
13	Miles Davis Jazz Series
14	Bill Evans Jazz Series

15

16

17

15 | *Flower Fairy Self Promotion*

16 | *Two Roses Self Promotion*

17 | *Star Goddess Self Promotion*

K o j i   N a k a m u r a

18

49

19

19

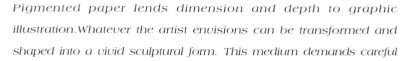

Pigmented paper lends dimension and depth to graphic illustration. Whatever the artist envisions can be transformed and shaped into a vivid sculptural form. This medium demands careful

PIGMENTED PAPER

planning and preparation. The color palette, whether rich and warm or wildly vivid, must be thoughtfully culled from the numerous papers available. Along with angles, curves and shadows each shade and tone becomes a dynamic element in the construction of the finished work. Cindy Berglund, Dee DeLoy and Mark Marturello each take a unique approach that fully realizes the potential of color variation in their expressive paper sculptures.

Berglund begins her work by exploring the limitless possibilities. This creative freedom is translated into striking sculptures through a long and complex assembly process. Richly layered, the work of DeLoy gives a sense of almost infinite depth. He strengthens this illusion through his modulation of the tonal range and manipulation of light and shadows. The colorfully exaggerated characters in Marturello's figurative illustrations are eye catching and whimsical. Foreshortened perspective, sharply scored paper bends and brightly contrasting colors give his work its visual appeal. The works of Berglund, DeLoy and Marturello demonstrate a singular style which has emerged from careful engineering and adventurous experimentation.

CINDY BERGLUND

Cindy Berglund has been perfecting her paper sculpture skills for the past 20 years. While working as an illustrator, she convinced several clients that paper sculpture was an ideal solution for solving special illustration problems. Berglund learned the art through trial and error, together with infinite hours of experimentation. She works with a variety of materials ranging from simple construction to embossed papers. Every project requires careful planning, meticulous precision and an abundance of patience. Since photography is an essential adjunct of the total illustration, she experiments with a variety of techniques designed to convey mood and dimension.

Work is created for all advertising, editorial and publication markets. Berglund's artistry has been honored by the 3Dimensional Art Directors and Illustrators Awards Show, Communication Arts, Print's Regional Design Annual and the New York Art Directors Club. Cindy confesses she enjoys the creative freedom and limitless possibilities of paper sculpture and feels, "at the end of all the hours of construction, something magical will appear. And it does!"

1 A sketch of the lilies is created on Bienfang 360 graphic paper for the original pencil layout. Copies of the drawing are made. Each part of the design is color coded and numbered with fine point markers to indicate all the pattern components.

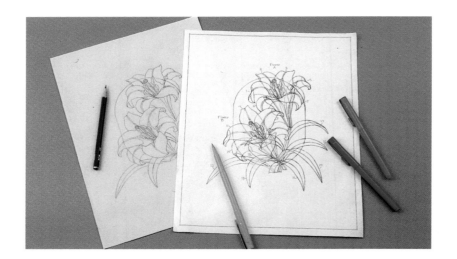

2 A color rendering is created using Berol Prismacolor markers. Pantone uncoated papers are chosen to match the color sketch closely. Starwhite Vicksburg (100lb.) Tiara white smooth text stock is selected for the petal flowers.

3 A second copy of the overall design is made. It is placed face down on the lightbox. The chosen papers are taped color-side-down on top of the layout. With a mechanical pencil, each element is traced onto the paper one at a time.

Intricate shapes are traced and cut free-hand with scissors to minimize the visibility of the white base of the pigmented paper. All the elements are cut out and grouped as flower #1 and flower #2. The leaves are coded to match the numbers on the layout to assure proper placement.

4

Using a #11 knife blade, the patterns are cut out on the lightbox. A piece of acetate is positioned under the paper (to allow direct cutting on the lightbox without damaging the original layout). A French curve and ellipse templates are used for precise shapes.

5

The leaves are gently scored down the middle. They are then folded inward using the thumbs and forefingers. The curl is formed by slowly rolling the paper over a round or hard edge of wood. A tighter roll is achieved by wrapping over a sharper edge. A softer effect is obtained by using a curved rim.

6

7 The center line on each piece is reversed scored into a piece of foamcore. A metal spoon burnisher is applied with a constant, even pressure. The surface texture of the pistil and stamen is obtained by gouging small pointed circles with the tip of the tool. This embossing technique gives depth and dimension to the sculpture.

8 The embossed petals are marked and coded by number. Spray adhesive is gently sprayed over the back of the yellow petal. It is then positioned on the white petal forming the flower. When joining the overlapping parts, assembly can be done on a lightbox using the layout as a visual guide.

9 Short pieces of transfer adhesive tape are cut. They are rolled into thick and thin strips. Sections of the roll are sliced off. Using the knife, they are placed in position affixing the darker toned leaves and flowers together. This adds depth and creates the illusion of a shadow. The tape offers some slight repositioning for adjustments when the sculpture is completed.

The pink oval is cut with the knife using the circle templates as a guide. A matching piece of sturdy white paper (with a slightly larger opening) is cut. The white paper is affixed to the pink oval giving stability and firmness. A bright blue paper is glued to the foamcore as a background. Foamcore spacers are used to join the two.

10

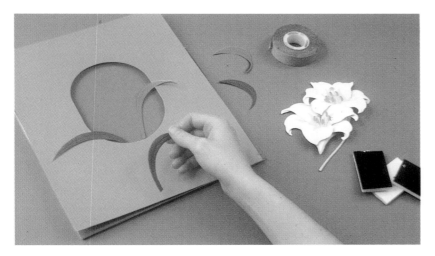

Each flower is completely assembled and placed in the oval. The remaining leaves are arranged around the outer edge in the oval. A clear acetate copy of the layout is positioned over the artwork to check for accuracy.

11

Final positioning of the design is implemented. The flowers are attached with transfer adhesive tape using foamcore spacers. With this process, proper lift and directional tilt are attained. The transfer tape allows for shifting and adjustments. Art direction of the sculpture is critical to the mood and expression of the artwork.

12

1 | Party With The Parrot Advertising Campaign

2 | Autumn Hunt Advertising Poster

3 | Bass Advertising Illustration

Cindy Berglund

59

7 Corporate Portrait Business Award

8 The Illustrators Workshop Does Paris Brochure Cover

9 Cinnamon Toast Crunch Guys Ring Binder Cover

60

Cindy Berglund

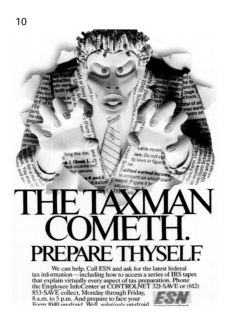

10 | *The Taxman Cometh Advertising Poster*

11 | *Tax Planning Brochure Cover*

12 | *Fidelity Investor Center Advertising Mailing*

13

15

14

Cindy Berglund

16

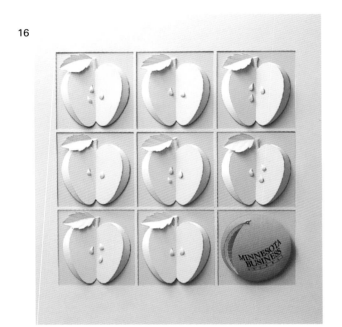

17

18

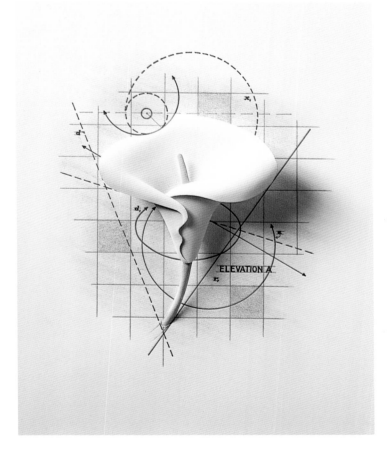

ELEVATION A

63

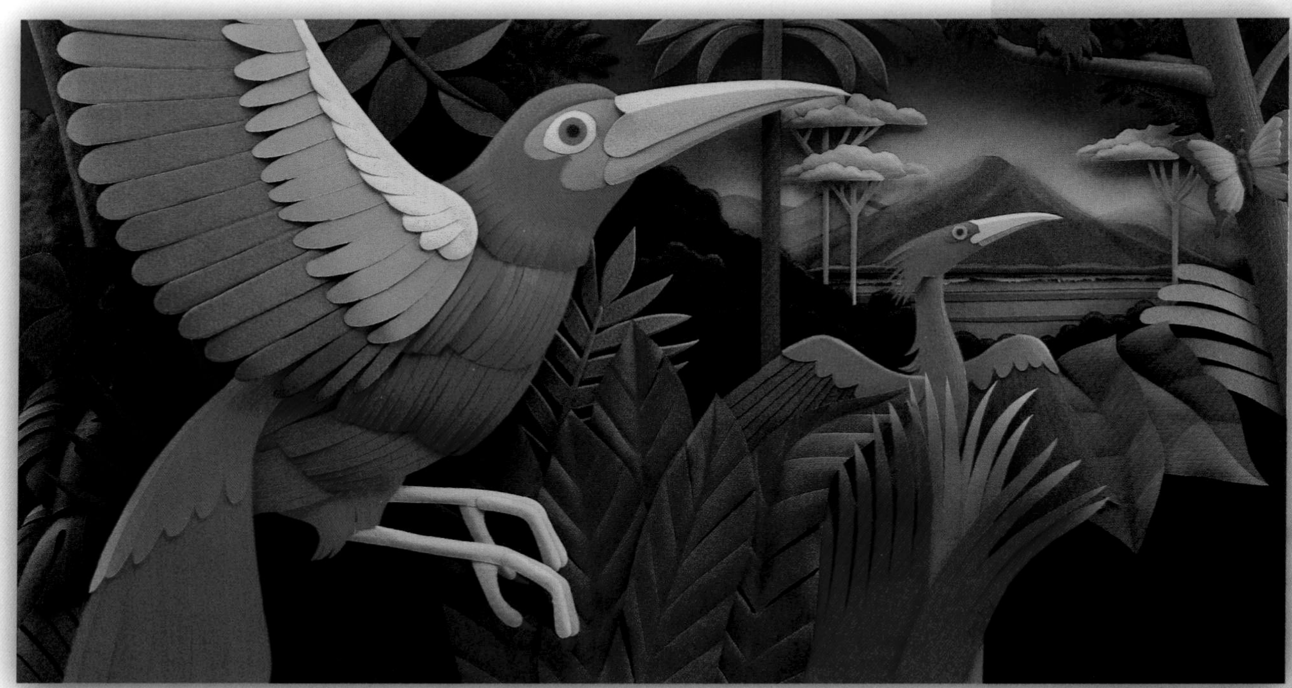

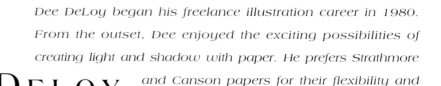

Dee DeLoy began his freelance illustration career in 1980. From the outset, Dee enjoyed the exciting possibilities of creating light and shadow with paper. He prefers Strathmore and Canson papers for their flexibility and durability. His dynamic signature style is energized by detail and color. Considered a purist, Dee occasionally airbrushes the paper with acrylic paint, or uses a sponge to enhance the color and texture. He works closely with a photographer and frequently experiments with new techniques to keep the work contemporary.

DEE DELOY

DeLoy's studio has a plethora of unique dental and sculptural tools designed to produce illustrations which are both visually appealing and creatively animated. He has received numerous accolades from the 3Dimensional Art Directors and Illustrators Awards Show, a first-place Addy award, and a Best of Show for a national promotional campaign. Specializing in corporate, advertising and publishing art, Dee enjoys the "trompe l'oeil effect of paper sculpture on the viewer."

1 A rough sketch of the jungle scene is drawn in blue pencil. Using a mechanical pencil, the drawing is then refined with elaborate details. An ellipse template is used to define the leaves and feathers.

2 The color palette is selected from a vivid assortment of stock papers. Small pieces are cut and placed together to test the tonal variations. This process is important in securing proper color harmony within the composition.

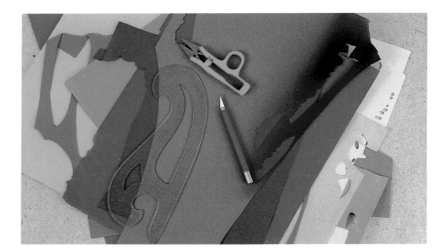

3 A section of the leaf is traced onto a scrap of translucent paper. It is placed face down on the moss green sheet. A burnishing tool is rubbed over the line, transferring the shape of the leaf to the colored paper.

Carefully following the transferred pencil line, each element is cut out with a #11 knife blade. The trimmed line is usually made larger than the original drawing. This allows for a change in the shape of the paper when it is curled and scored.

4

After the leaves are cut out they are then scored. Using the knife, the blade is dragged down the center of the leaf. Care is taken to prevent the paper from being sliced through all the way. It is then gently bent between the fingers to form the score fold. The leaf shapes are then burnished on the back to create the curve.

5

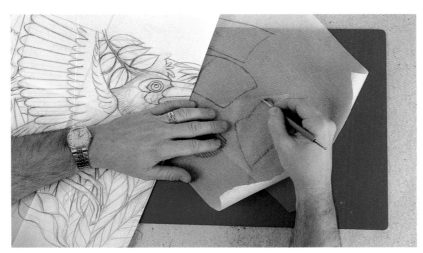

A tracing is made of the bird section from the original drawing. The shape is transferred to the back of the red paper by burnishing the tracing paper face down.

6

7 The colorful wings and body are individually cut out. Vertical slices are made on the front shaped sections to give a feathered effect. Using a plastic tool, the pieces are molded from behind to form a soft curl.

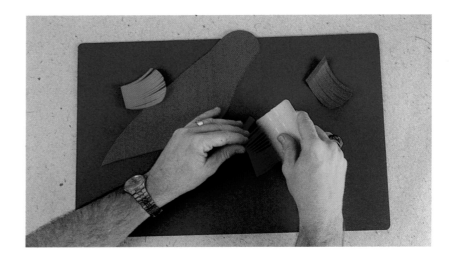

8 The feathers are then affixed to the main bird base shape. The legs are assembled underneath the entire construction. White water-based, acid-free glue is applied for permanency. Foamcore spacers are used to support the layers of the structure.

9 A piece of foamcore is cut for the large wing support. Vertical slices are made in the blue, green and yellow sections. They are attached with glue to the foamcore base. The outer wing is then positioned in place with tweezers and joined to the body

Dee DeLoy

The landscape created from flat paper is fastened on a foamcore background. The smaller trees are attached in place first. Foamcore spacers are positioned behind the foliage leaves for added depth.

10

After the foliage leaves are cut and scored, they are further curled using the handle of a paintbrush. Foamcore spacers are constructed higher for the foreground pieces. The leaves are affixed with white acid-free glue. Slight adjustments are made while the adhesive is drying.

11

All the assembled pieces are fastened in place, layer by layer. The completed bird is positioned and attached with glue to the high foamcore spacers. This adds depth and dimension to the entire image. Some final adjustments are made curving the leaf and wing forms. The finished artwork is then photographed with precise lighting.

12

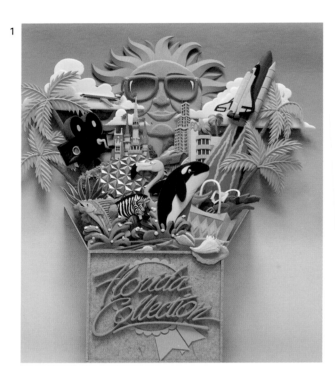

1

3

2

Dee DeLoy

4 | *Birthday Mickey Poster ©1997 Walt Disney Co.*

5 | *Theme Parks In The Sky Christmas Card*
    ©1997 Walt Disney Co.

6 | *Where Dreams Take Flight Poster*

D e e   D e L o y

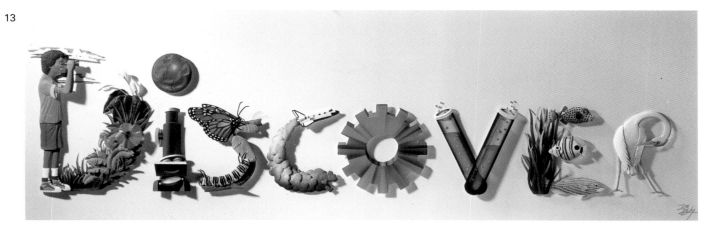

14

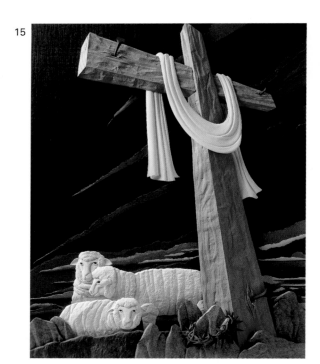

15

16

D e e   D e L o y

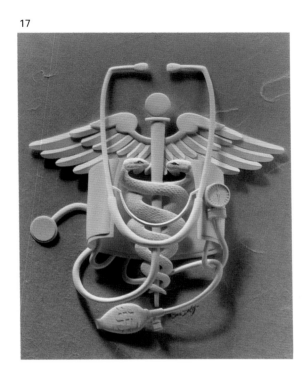

MARK MARTURELLO

Mark Marturello, best known for his stylized characters, is a self-taught paper sculptor, presently working for the Des Moines Register. Paper sculpture affords him the opportunity to bring life to his illustrations. His endearing caricatures are examples of his singular style. He prefers working with Canson construction paper because it provides a spectrum of colors, textures and weights. His strength lies in the interpretation of people and gesture.

Marturello's illustrations appear primarily in newspapers and magazines. His whimsical paper sculptures have earned him many accolades including top awards in the American Illustrations Annuals 14, and 15, the Society of Newspaper Design, and the 3Dimensional Art Directors and Illustrators Awards Show. He believes that paper sculpture captures and holds the imagination of the viewer more than traditional flat illustration. And, he enjoys the medium because it gives him license to express his ideas dimensionally. "Paper sculpture is a genuine attention getter. It gives me an extra freedom to communicate, and a satisfaction that I get from no other technique."

1 A concept for the paper sculpture is created depicting two people sitting on top of a house with a fish-eye perspective. Preliminary drawings are made of the figures and house scene in pencil. The shapes are then refined with more detail.

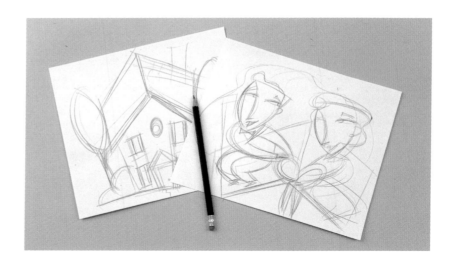

2 Canson construction paper is selected because of its textural surface. Rainbow shades of laser paper are preferred because of their tonal gradation. This eliminates the need to airbrush the background.

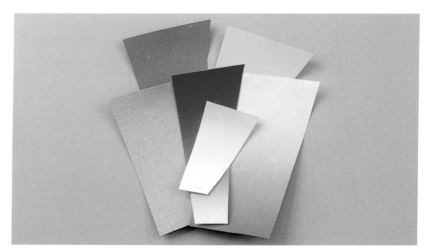

3 Several copies are made of the initial sketches. Graphite is applied to the back to make a carbon transfer sheet. The copy is then placed on top of the selected paper and the exact shapes are redrawn.

Mark Marturello

Using the pale Canson construction paper, the drawing of the face is transferred to the back. The head shape is carefully cut out using a #11 knife blade. Several sections of the face are made because they will be positioned in layers.

4

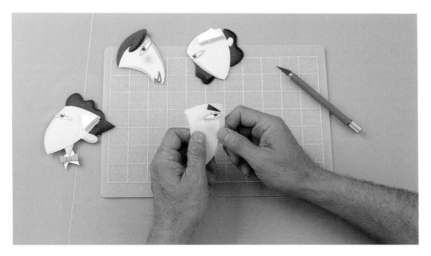

After all the pieces are cut they are formed to create character and give depth to the facial features. Using a #11 blade, a light score is made down the side of the head. The paper is then bent along the score. The hair and eyes are then attached.

5

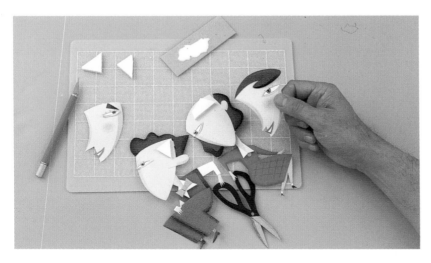

Once the scores are implemented, the entire construction is assembled. Pieces of foamcore are cut as spacers. They are then glued in position between the layers to add dimension to the face. The figures are then adhered to the body shapes.

6

7 The house is fabricated from a white base with yellow Canson paper as the clapboard. A small dormer with columns is constructed in a foreshortened perspective. It is then attached over the door.

8 Variations of blue laser gradation paper are selected. Small strips are placed behind the window openings to compare the best match. A light tonal range is chosen for the windows and then taped on the back.

9 The roof is built from brown Canson construction paper. A score is made down the center and it is folded in half, creating the pitch. The shingles are made by cutting three small slices on the surface and bending the paper up slightly. This is done in a random pattern, giving the impression of a shingled roof.

Mark Marturello

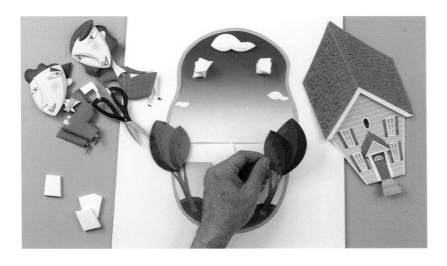

An oval is cut from the blue gradation laser paper for the sky background. Trees are made from simple round shapes and scored once. They are attached on the base and glued in position in the foreground.

10

Several pieces of foamcore are cut and affixed together. They are stacked to an adequate height for the house and fastened with white glue to the background. The entire assembly is then attached onto the foam spacers.

11

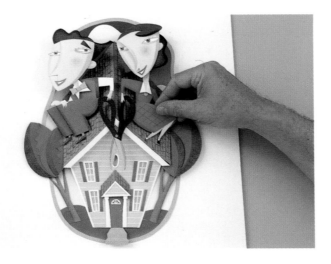

After the glue dries, the trees are adjusted around the side of the house. A stack of foamcore spacers are made. They are positioned in the sky background. The completed assembly of figures is attached in place. Additional foam pieces are strategically added for additional support.

12

81

1

2

3

1 | Bird Watching Newspaper Editorial

2 | Instant Meal Newspaper Editorial

3 | White Men Can't Dance Newspaper Editorial

Mark Marturello

84

7

9

8

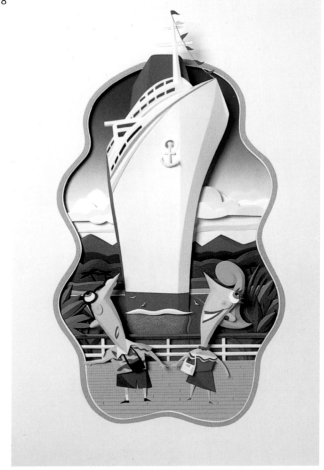

10

Mark Marturello

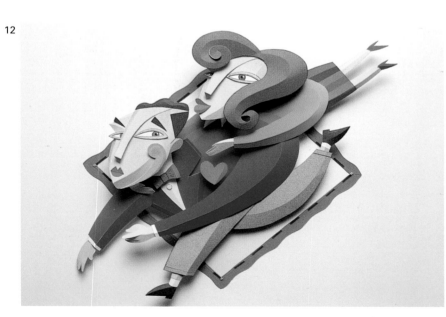

11 | *Wedding Wee-pers Newspaper Editorial*

12 | *Fatal Attraction Newspaper Editorial*

13 | *Housing Outlook Newspaper Editorial*

14

15

16

14 | *Bad Dog Newspaper Editorial*

15 | *Bridges of Edison Crowley Newspaper Editorial*

16 | *Gothic Gardening Newspaper Editorial*

Mark Marturello

18

17

17 | *Silent Scream Illustration*

18 | *Eye For An Eye Illustration*

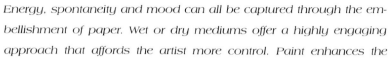

EMBELLISHED PAPER

Energy, spontaneity and mood can all be captured through the embellishment of paper. Wet or dry mediums offer a highly engaging approach that affords the artist more control. Paint enhances the texture, volume and dimension of the paper; pastel and colored pencil soften the contours and shapes of the edges. These applications push the sculpting process further—allowing for subtle nuance, trompe l'oeil, and emotional gesture. The techniques used to apply color to paper are diverse. The work of Marcelo Bicalho, Pat Allen and Ricardo Radosh show how gouache, watercolor, acrylics, paint, pencils and pastels can all be utilized to create a provocative range of sensation and depth.

With an unfamiliar angle of view and a sense of action in progress, Bicalho lures us into his imaginary world. Detailed expressionism is found in his combination of papers with painting and printing methods. Allen prefers adding surface texture to her prized collection of papers. Delicate layering of spattered paint and a rich tonal palette give the work a warm and enticing quality. Paper sculpture allows Radosh to hold the viewer's attention while addressing difficult subjects. In his artwork, he uses colored pencil to create visual tension, emphasize drama and stir empathy. The versatility of the medium allows each artist to find their own distinct technique and then develop their own creative style.

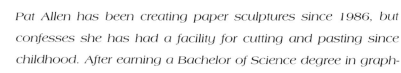

PAT ALLEN

Pat Allen has been creating paper sculptures since 1986, but confesses she has had a facility for cutting and pasting since childhood. After earning a Bachelor of Science degree in graphic design, she began her career working in a studio, producing medical and technical sculptures for annual reports. Encouraged by her clients and agent, she began as a freelance paper sculptor. She prefers papers with a high cotton content, since they provide the highest amount of flexibility. Most of her pieces include decorative papers from her extensive collection which she embellishes with sponging, spattering and painting techniques.

Her work has received many awards from the 3Dimensional Art Directors and Illustrators Awards Show, the Art Directors Club of Los Angeles, Illustration West and Print Magazine. She attempts to create new challenges within each project that will enhance her knowledge and skills of paper sculpture. Allen regards this medium as the perfect solution for solving illustration problems. "It's really exciting when I can match an exquisite piece of paper to the perfect application. Paper sculpture, as illustration, has the power to capture the viewer's attention through its rich dimensional qualities."

1 Currents, an in-house magazine, commissioned this paper sculpture cover to illustrate a new company concept in ready-to-eat groceries. The idea is to construct a shopping bag depicting the cooked food possibilities. After several sketches are created, a final drawing is made.

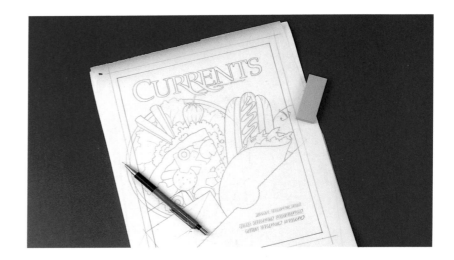

2 Although Canson Mi-Teintes is most often used, selections are chosen from a wide variety of commercial and handmade papers that have been acquired over the years. Specific papers are matched to each item created. Japanese Kyo-sei was chosen for the lettuce, Colombe was selected for the cottage cheese and Larroque was preferred for the taco shell, pepperoni and pizza crust.

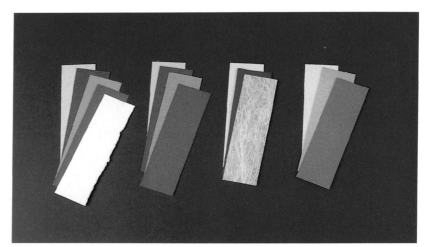

3 Intricate patterns are drawn for each element and copies are made. A light application of one-coat cement is brushed onto the back of the copy. For ease of folding and curling, the pattern is affixed to the paper in the direction of the grain.

P a t   A l l e n

A light coating of cement is applied to the back of the hotdog bun pattern. Consideration is given to the direction of the grain and where the folds and curls are located. Using a number #11 blade, the shape is cut along the outer lines. After the piece is cut, folds are made with a scoring tool.

The pepperoni and olive slices are cut out with a circle guide. The mushroom is cut freehand, and painted to suggest texture and shadow. Various brush strokes of paint are delicately applied to the pepperoni slice to render a realistic surface.

After the papers are washed with paint they are cut using a pattern. White glue is applied to the back of the circles. While still damp, the pieces are rolled and pinched with the fingers to form the taco shape. After drying, the edges are trimmed and painted.

93

7 Red paper is cut for the apple using the patterns. After burnishing the surface, the paper is worked with the fingers and the apple begins to take shape. Thin strips are applied to the darts joining the sides together. After each strip dries, they are burnished lightly along the seam to smooth the curves.

8 The pattern is carefully removed and the bun is formed by rolling the paper into a curved shape with the fingers. The burnisher is used to further round the paper. The tabs are adhered with glue to the back of the bun to secure the shape.

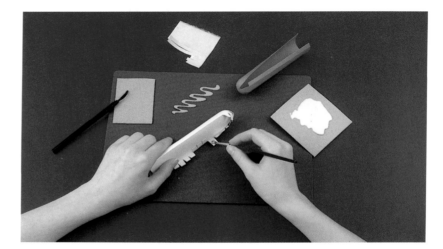

9 The papers are painted with diverse textures and colors. A light wash of thinned paint is applied to the taco and pepperoni papers. They are then speckled with a paint soaked toothbrush. The lettuce is created by airbrushing at a slight angle to retain the texture and to let some of the white show through. Paint that resembles a stone texture is sprayed on the background blue paper.

Pat Allen

The elements are assembled in position to check for accuracy. Before gluing, a light coat of paint is air-brushed on the hotdog bun and pizza slice. This embellishment adds a toasted look to the food and a colorful dimension to the pieces.

10

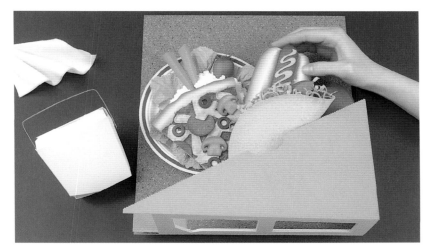

The background blue textured paper is adhered to a foamcore board. A facsimile of a brown bag is constructed with foam spacers. After assembling the salad, the entire section is the first piece to be glued down. The pizza is bonded to the top of the salad. The apple is juxtaposed on the upper edge of the bag and the hotdog is fastened in place.

11

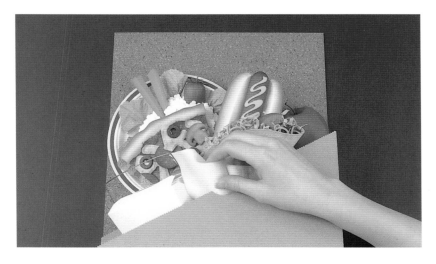

The Chinese take-out container is slipped into position. A dinner-size napkin is trimmed in half and then taped to create soft-accordion folds. Final adjustments to the sculpture are made by twisting the ends of the paper edges.

12

1

96

2

3

Semiconductor Equipment Materials International

1 | *Boston Campaign Series*

2 | *Geneva Campaign Series*

3 | *San Francisco Campaign Series*

Pat Allen

4

5

6

Semiconductor Equipment Materials International

4	*Tokyo Campaign Series*
5	*Kyoto Campaign Series*
6	*Seoul Campaign Series*

7

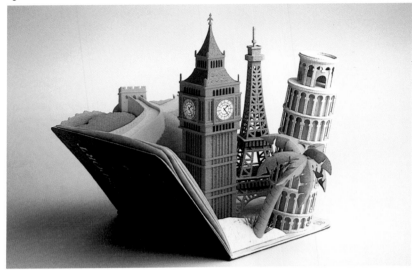

9

8

7 | Stock Certificate Advertisement

8 | International Investing Advertisement

9 | Passport Advertisement

P a t   A l l e n

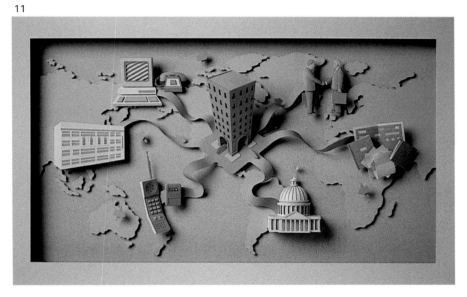

13

14

15

Pat Allen

16

18

17

16	*Timber Wolf Advertisement*
17	*Predator Advertisement*
18	*Jungle Predators Advertisement*

RICARDO RADOSH

Ricardo Radosh began his career in Mexico as a traditional graphic illustrator working with two-dimensional wet and dry media. In 1990, he experimented with paper cut-outs and discovered that paper sculpture offered him limitless creative opportunities. Radosh finds "something special" in paper and will use whatever is available to create a sculpture. He embellishes the sheets with watercolors, acrylics and gouaches, and uses colored pencils and pastels to add depth and texture. His studio includes the usual array of tools, but he also works with sharp Chinese scissors for very precise cuts. He creates his work primarily for the editorial market. His signature style graphically depicts the powerful satirical imagery of the political and economic issues of Mexico.

Radosh understands the important implications of his work and wishes to impact on the social and political climate of the nation. He has won awards for paper sculpture from the Codigram College of Mexican Industrial and Graphic Designers and the 3Dimensional Art Directors and Illustrators Awards Show. Radosh enjoys the freedom and versatility of paper sculpture because, "it allows me the possibility of achieving striking images with unlimited creativity and lots of room for improvisation."

1 Initial, concepts are created to design the composition. More refined sketches for the hummingbird and flowers are then drawn. After finalizing all the shapes, a detailed drawing is rendered with a fine-point marker.

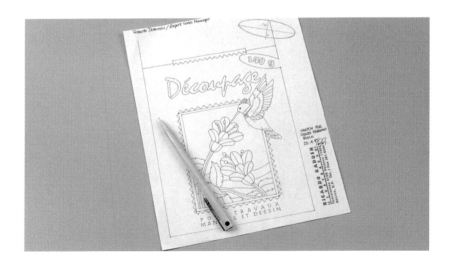

2 The image is to be used for Fabriano Color Construction paper, block cover. Selections are made from actual samples found in the block. Many colors are chosen to showcase the paper in the illustrated cover.

3 The final sketch of the hummingbird and flowers is placed on the lightbox. A pencil tracing is made of all the separate pieces. The selected paper is then put on the lightbox and an outline tracing of each shape is drawn on the back.

Ricardo Radosh

The flower petals are cut with a rotating fine blade. The details of the flower and hummingbird are made with Chinese scissors. Pencil lines are used as a guide but a great deal of improvisation is implemented for the actual shapes. After cutting, the parts are placed on the sketch to check for proper size and form.

4

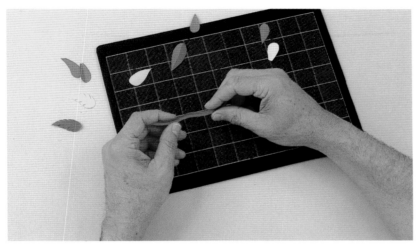

Once the parts are completely cut out, the petals, leaves and stems are scored. Using a sharp blade, a score is made down the middle of each piece, just deep enough to cut the thickness of the paper in half. Extreme care is taken to prevent the paper from being cut all the way through. It is folded along the scored line with the thumbs.

5

Since the Fabriano is very flat, colored pencils are used to add texture. Crosshatching lines are made along the edge of the scored fold, enhancing the dimension and form of the sculpture.

6

7 White glue is applied in a used candy dispenser. The petals and leaves are positioned carefully along the stem and set in place over the drawing. All the petals are then fastened from the base to the top in an over-lapping fashion. The leaves are delicately affixed in place on the stem.

8 The "Decoupage" text is traced from a lightbox onto white Fabriano paper. Five extra layers are adhered with spray adhesive to give the text height. Each layer is cut out entirely with the rotating knife blade.

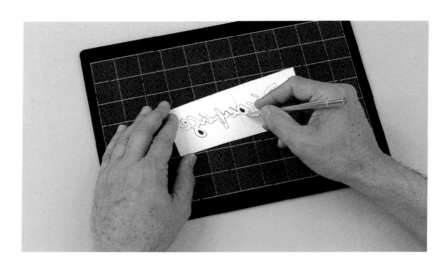

9 Brown and black paper are alternately reverse scored and folded to create an accordion shape. White pencil is added for shading and depth. The window frame is traced with rulers making the zigzag form. Each layer is joined with spray glue.

Ricardo Radosh

The window border is assembled to a foamcore board for height. The brown and black background is attached to a support base. The flowers are positioned with respect to the window opening. Throughout the gluing process, the border is placed on top to check the visibility through the opening.

10

A small triangular piece of cardboard is placed on the front surface of the purple paper. The hummingbird is then laid on top in various positions until the desired angle is achieved. The small board gives the bird height and adds dimension to the sculpture.

11

The bird is fastened in position. A small amount of glue is used to prevent it from seeping to the front surface of the purple paper. Final adjustments are made to the sculpture, making sure that the elements are securely in place.

12

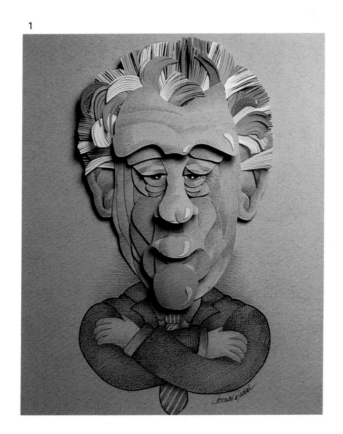

Ricardo Radosh

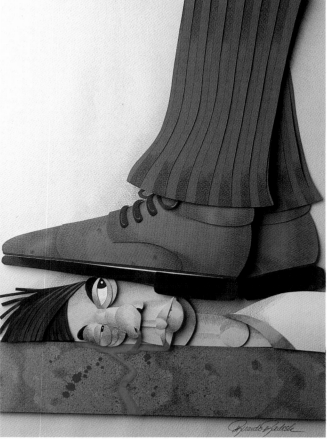

4	*Woody Allen Self Promotional Calendar*
5	*Victims Cover* *Political Supplement Newspaper*
6	*Genius Self Promotional Calendar*

7

8

9

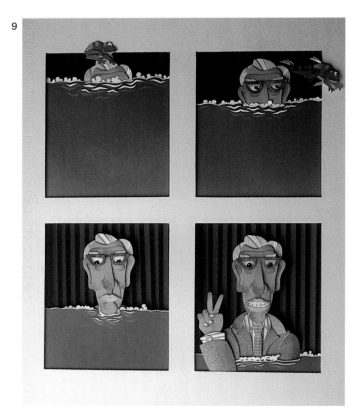

R i c a r d o   R a d o s h

R i c a r d o R a d o s h

16

1 1 3

17

18

MARCELO BICALHO

Marcelo Bicalho is a self-taught paper sculptor working in Belo Horizonte, Brazil. He believes paper is the ideal medium to express his personal approach and style of illustration. He uses an assortment of colors and surfaces, but prefers Canson Papers for their flexibility and texture. Bicalho adds textural painted embellishments using watercolors and gouaches with brushes, sponges or toothbrush. Elongated figures and warped perspective characterize his singular style.

His paper sculptures are primarily designed for the advertising and editorial markets. Marcelo's imagery has appeared in many of Brazil's leading periodicals. In 1996, he was honored with a Bronze Award from the 3Dimensional Art Directors and Illustrators Awards Show. He creates in paper because it affords the opportunity to express his spontaneity. "Paper unites the various facets of my work and offers me the freedom to create the perfect illustrative solution."

1 First rough individual sketches of a circus scene are created. The elements are then transferred to a larger paper through a lightbox. Each component is positioned to create a harmonious composition. The final drawing is then refined with the exact details of all the characters.

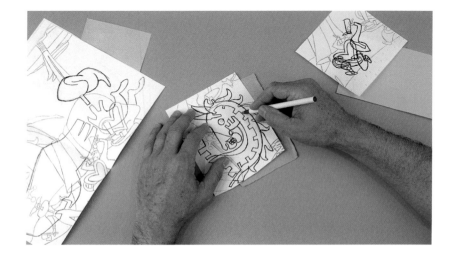

2 Commercial and handmade papers are embellished with spatter, printing and painting techniques. Pink and cream Canson papers are sprayed with a thin layer of silver paint for the horse's body. Silver gouache is mixed in the godet and brushed on the white Canson sheet for the acrobatic ballerina. Handmade proof prints are chosen for the tuba man's pants and the drummer's hat. Recycled paper, made by the artist's son is also selected.

3 Many photocopies are made of each element in the design. The images are pressed into the paper by tracing over the outline in ballpoint pen. An exact, blind embossed line is defined, indicating the edges that will attach to the adjoining piece. The color of the pen is important to differentiate the lines drawn from the basic sketch.

The inside contours are cut with a #11 blade following the blind embossed lines. They are changed frequently to ensure a clean, precise slice. Outside shapes are cut with a small sharp scissor. A luminous torch is used to emphasize the little furrows along the edge.

The sides are rounded to create a soft edge. Using an opened paper clip, the paper is curled gently. Patience and a delicate hand are needed to produce a homogeneous quality to the edges. Undesirable points can be cut off carefully with a scissor.

1 **1** 7

Photocopies are used to arrange the pieces in the correct position. The elements are adhered with transparent glue using the drawing as a guide. Each part is attached by putting a small amount of glue on the tabs. The tabs securely interlock the shapes together.

7 Additional embellishing is added to the figures. The hair and face of the fire-eating man are painted with a small brush in brown watercolor The stripes on his pants are rendered with a pointed silver quick-dry marker. Tiny dots are added to the hat and the pants of the drum player.

8 The locks that were included on the image fasten the pieces that are fabricated from multiple parts. The glue helps to keep the entire assemblage together. After it dries, the zeppelin is gently formed into a gentle curve with the fingers and thumbs.

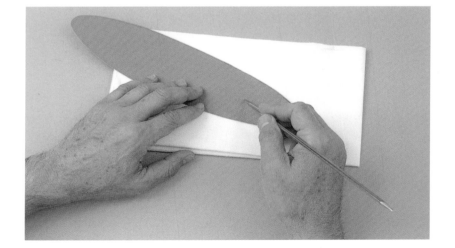

9 The carpet is cut from green Canson paper and placed on several layers of folded fabric. A relief technique is applied by pressing a rounded point or needle into the surface to create an overall embossed texture. Care is taken to prevent the tip from piercing the paper.

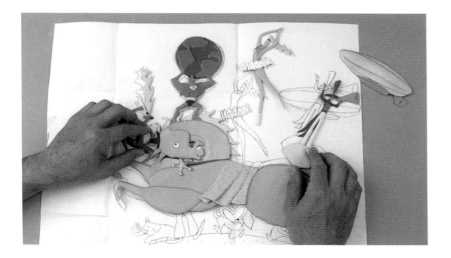

The horse assembly is positioned on the initial final sketch. Once the desired placement is achieved, the figures are carefully hot glued to the horse using folded strips of paper as support. Wire is used to brace the strong man and globe.

10

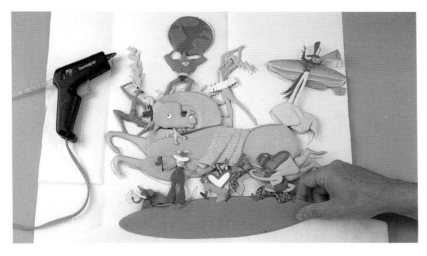

The green carpet is glued to a stiff translucent paper, made from white fiber and resin. All the characters are then attached to the carpet. The entire construction is fastened to the horse assemblage and then to a styrofoam. Wire supports are passed behind the tuba man and into the foam board.

11

The zeppelin is glued to a strip of paper and affixed to the tall man with the blue hat. The wire support behind the tuba player is attached to secure both the tall man and the zeppelin.

12

1 | *Formato Editorial Book Illustration*

2 | *Formato Editorial Book Illustration*

Marcelo Bicalho

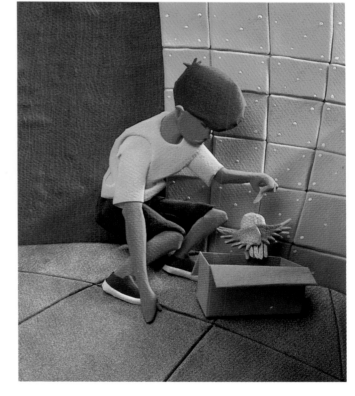

3 | *Formato Editorial Book Illustration*

4 | *Formato Editorial Book Illustration*

5 | *Saúde Magazine Illustration*

6 | *Geração Editorial Book Cover*

7 | *Bovespa Magazine Cover*

M a r c e l o   B i c a l h o

8

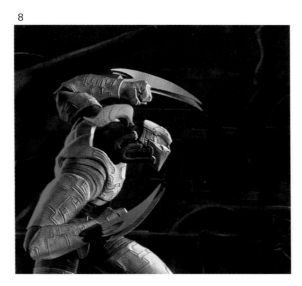

9

10

1 **2** 3

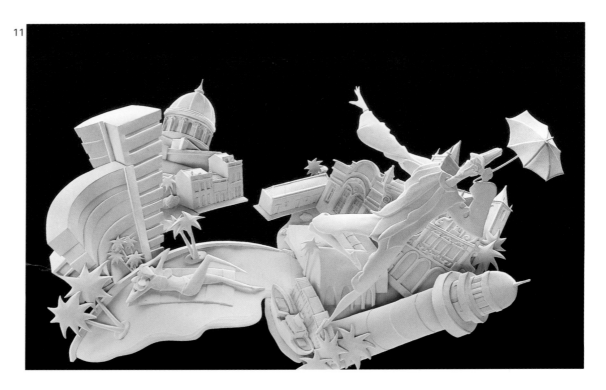

11 | Credicard Event Invitation Folder

12 | Playboy Magazine Illustration

Marcelo Bicalho

1 **2** 5

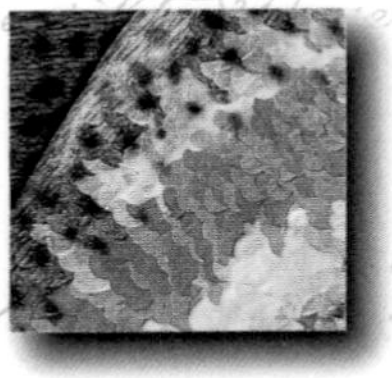

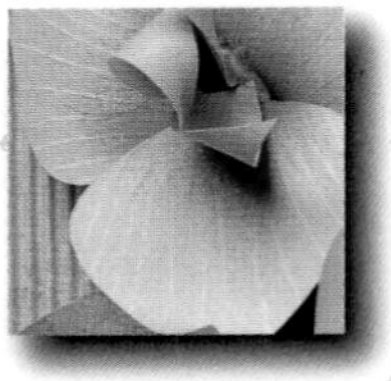

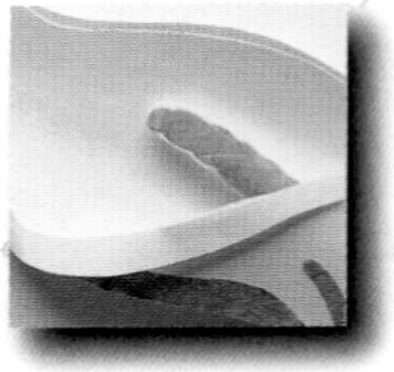

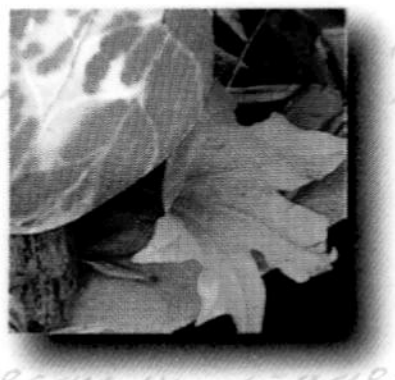

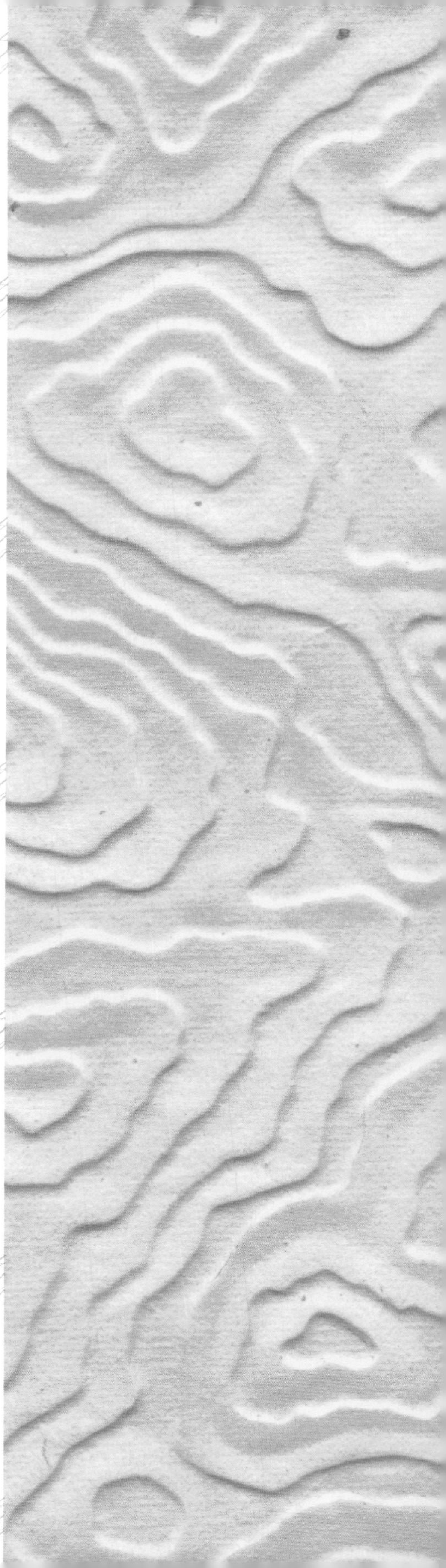

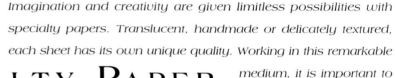

SPECIALTY PAPER

Imagination and creativity are given limitless possibilities with specialty papers. Translucent, handmade or delicately textured, each sheet has its own unique quality. Working in this remarkable medium, it is important to recognize the structural and metaphoric potential of each paper. Eastern and Western hand-formed sheets offer an inspirational assortment of fibers and pigments.

Thoughtful and original, the work of both Joan Kritchman-Knuteson and Carol Jeanotilla demonstrates the versatility of paper as an illustrative medium. Each has taken a highly personal approach with uncommon and refreshing results. Jeanotilla nurtures her projects by reflecting on the paper while envisioning the outcome. She focuses on bold colors, the relationship of surfaces, and strong textures. Her sculptures have a striking graphic feel. Interpretation of nature is an essential component of Kritchman-Knuteson's visual style. She relies on a deep awareness of subtle color, opacity and shadow. Working with layers and tissue-thin sheets allows her to create a sense of depth and fluidity. Graceful and highly detailed, their artistry reflects a concern for harmony and balance. Each artist uses this distinct genre to captivate and dazzle the viewer.

JOAN KRITCHMAN-KNUTESON

Joan Kritchman-Knuteson's career as a paper sculptor began in 1974. Her technical acumen, dimensional perspective and appreciation of nature are characteristics of her unique style. Kritchman-Knuteson prefers working with acid-free or rag-mixed papers because they resist fading and chipping. For commissioned pieces, she selects rag-mixed papers because of their flexibility and durability. Sponging, airbrushing and spattering with a toothbrush are the techniques used for adding color, depth and texture.

Joan divides her work equally between advertising and commissioned pieces. The subtle textures reflect a love of nature. Many of the sculptures contain a Far Eastern motif. Recognized for her paper sculpture illustrations by the 3Dimensional Art Directors and Illustrators Awards Show, Joan's work is displayed in advertisements, magazines and galleries, throughout the country. She prefers paper sculpture because it enables the artist to manipulate light, shadow and depth. Joan believes "creating with paper is like painting dimensionally."

1   Using her extensive morgue reference file, ideas are generated for the grapevine composition. A tight color sketch is rendered in marker. The visual layout assists in achieving color scheme possibilities.

2   Once the sketch is finalized, the papers are selected. Consideration is given as to how well the patterns and surface textures work harmoniously. Papers with neutral Ph and rag are chosen including: Japanese Ogura and Unryu't, blue and maroon marbled, as well as Fabriano, Richard De Bas and French printmaking papers.

3   Copies are made of the initial sketch and one-coat cement is applied to the back. This gives enough tack (without too much adhesion) and prevents damage to the paper when it is removed. This is especially important with the lighter rice papers. Using a #11 knife blade, each shape is cut. A small scissor is then used to feather notches in the leaves.

Joan Kritchman-Knuteson

Various leaves are cut out of brown, green and rust papers. After the pattern is removed, a score line is made bisecting the leaf, simulating the natural vein. Forward and reverse scores are created on the front and back. Care is taken to prevent the paper from being cut too deep.

4

Paint is embellished on the leaves to add more interest and to create a feeling of the foliage turning color. A natural sponge is used to apply complementary colors to the surface. A smaller texture is implemented by spattering paint from the tips of a toothbrush.

5

1 **3** 1

Vines are cut from the pattern copies. The tendrils are then made from thin strips of paper. The strips are wrapped around a brush handle to fabricate the spiral effect. Using a smaller diameter brush will make a tighter curl; a larger diameter will achieve a bigger curl. As the vines are completed, individual tendrils are attached to the little leaves.

6

7 The base of the grape clusters are cut from the dark blue marbled paper. Each cluster is built up in layers with the lightest color on top. The individual grapes are traced from a circle template, from the maroon and blue marbled papers and the light blue rice paper. Pieces of foamcore are inserted between each layer to raise the depth of the overall shape.

8 The small grape clusters are glued to the larger base. Working inward toward the center, the lightest layers are affixed last. Clothespins are used to clamp the assemblage. The varying heights add more depth and give the illusion of roundness.

9 Lattice strips are cut from micro-veneer wood. They are glued to foamcore for support. The assembled vines are adhered on the structure. A cream-colored piece of rice paper is attached to a foamboard for the background, and the entire framework is fastened on top.

Joan Kritchman-Knuteson

The sculpture is constructed by positioning the bottom layers on the background. Leaves that are the farthest away are affixed first. The grape assemblages are attached to the vines. The large leaves are then arranged in place.

10

The mat is cut from acid-free board. For decoration, thin micro-veneer wood strips are joined to the perimeter of the opening. Marbled paper strips are placed inside the mat to harmonize the composition. Wide foamcore strips are trimmed and positioned underneath the edge of the board to separate the mat from the base.

11

1 **3** 3

The completed mat is put in position over the foamcore base. Final leaves are attached to the frame, thereby giving a cohesive appearance to the entire sculpture. This also adds to the illusion of dimension. Adjustments are then made, and shapes are arranged as needed.

12

1 **3** 4

3

2

4

6

8

7

6 | *Roses Fine Art*

7 | *Daisies Fine Art*

8 | *Calla Lilies Fine Art*

9 | *TriBond Game Box Cover*

10 | *Zebra Carrousel Animal Fine Art*

11 | *Phoenix Editorial*

12

13

14

12	Moonlight & Shadow Wolves Fine Art
13	Chameleon Fine Art
14	Cool Dude Basset Hound Fine Art

Joan Kritchman-Knuteson

CAROL JEANOTILLA

Paper sculpture has been a magical medium for Carol Jeanotilla. In 1990, her career as an illustrator and designer was threatened by the effects of multiple sclerosis. Paper sculpture afforded her the opportunity to use her hands in a uniquely creative medium. Jeanotilla became so successful as a paper sculptor, that she credits it with saving her commercial art career. While most artists rely on a pencil sketch to draft a concept, she creates a mental blueprint. This imaging process can take days, weeks and even years but, once completed, she continues working until the piece matches her vision. She believes strongly that the paper quality is paramount, and has paid as much as one-hundred dollars for a single sheet of paper. Hand-made papers are used for their overall texture and tensile strength; but quality, color-fast paper is preferred to insure the longevity of gallery work. She is convinced that photography contributes immensely to the total appeal of the sculpture.

Jeanotilla has been recognized for her paper sculpture artistry by the 3Dimensional Art Directors and Illustrators Awards Show, the National Touchstone Awards, the Healthcare Forum and the Art Directors Club of Denver. "Paper Sculpture is the embodiment of human emotions for me. If someone takes the time to look, all the pieces reflect the mirror image of my soul."

1 In place of a sketch, visual images are formed exploring through floral books. This visualization process takes a few days or weeks. Consideration is given to the purpose of the work in conjunction with textures and shapes to convey the appropriate message.

2 The papers are chosen after the images are mentally visualized. Texture and character of the sheet are matched to the mood of the piece. This is a critical stage that could last more than the actual time needed to construct the sculpture. A variety of handmade rag papers are selected that include Strathmore cover stock, textured Wyndstone, translucent rice and mulberry papers.

3 The composition is determined by arranging small pieces of the preferred paper into the desired design. A balance is achieved between the large white and violet papers for the iris, the orange paper for the tiger lily and the pink paper for the tulip.

Carol Jeanotilla

The largest flower, a tiger lily, is cut first. A light pencil line is made, on the orange paper as a guide. The length of each petal is the same but the curves vary, to simulate nature. After each piece is cut out using a #11 knife blade, press-on dots are placed in order of size starting at the tip. The petals are then glued together at the base and overlapped. A spiraling stamen is also added.

Without the use of a sketch, the daffodil is cut from brightly pigmented papers. The symmetrical creases of the petals are formed by rolling the paper around a pencil. By pressing firmly along the angled sides, the paper accepts the slight linear folds.

The clematis is formed in two parts. The leaves are cut out symmetrically from green textured paper. Using a brush handle, they are curled on the back and in the center. The flower is made from bright pink paper with natural shaped petals.

7 To construct the tulip, two petals are each cut out of one piece of paper leaving the base attached. The petals are rolled around a brush handle to form the curved shape. The four petals are then positioned overlapping on the base. A small amount of white glue is used to adhere the tulip together. Spiral stamens are made from very thin strips of paper and are glued deep inside the flower.

8 A basic pattern for the forget-me-not flower is drawn in pencil. It is then cut out and used as a template for the petals. After the flowers are cut, the edges are curled with the end of a brush to form a little triangle shape at the end of each petal. Small black and orange paper dots are punched out for the center.

9 The iris is constructed around a foamcore slice. It is placed in the clip stand and the large white petals are affixed with a glue gun. Three violet petals are cut free form with scissors, curved and fastened around the base of the white petals. The orange ruffle is made with scissor cuts and then attached last.

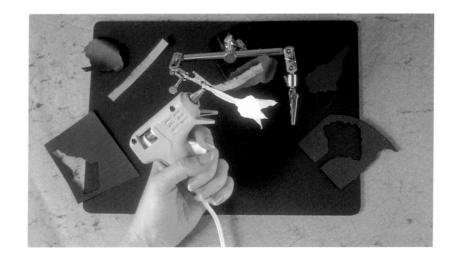

After all the flowers are completed, each one is inspected for details. Rough edges are trimmed and any remaining glue residue removed. The flowers are just placed in position first on the background to define the design. Many variations are considered before the final composition is set.

10

The completed leaves are then affixed on the black and white background first. The largest flowers, the lily and daffodil, are then attached. The placement of the pieces is determined by the negative space. To create a more natural effect, the pieces are glued in layers to vary the heights.

11

1 **4** 5

Once the major flowers are in place, the unsightly spaces are filled with smaller leaves. The petals are reshaped gently by curling with the fingers. Any remaining glue strands are discarded. The final arrangement is blown with compressed air to check for any loose pieces.

12

1

1 | Wild Trillium Fine Art Gallery Commission

2 | Dogwood Fine Art Gallery Commission

3 | Trillium Southampton Hospital

Carol Jeanotilla

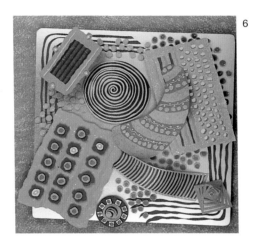

1 4 7

7

9

8

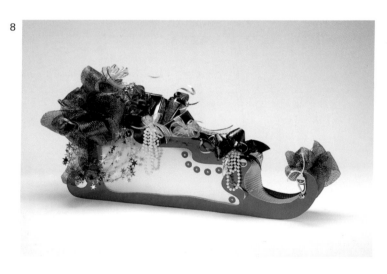

Carol Jeanotilla

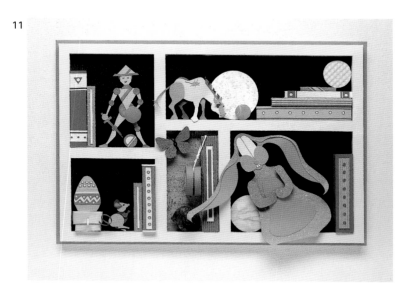

1 4 9

13

14

15

Carol Jeanotilla

ARTIST'S RIGHTS

Understanding the artist's rights of sale is an important ingredient for successful marketing and copyright protection. The paper sculptor has two distinct viable markets to consider, photographed paper sculpture used in print and original works of art sold as fine art. Each area can provide a lucrative source of income for the serious paper sculpture professional, but copyright protection is imperative.

For paper sculptures sold for use in print advertising and editorial, fees vary according to illustration size and print distribution. First time rights would permit the buyer to use the artwork one time per reproduction, as per the negotiated fee. Additional fees are paid for each usage thereafter. A contract between the creator of the work and the purchaser should determine the specific rights being transferred. These rights and the value of such rights should be included in the contract. All rights not transferred in the agreement remain the exclusive rights of the artist.

In addition, before photographing a work for print use, an agreement must be signed between the photographer and the paper sculptor. This contract should outline the shared rights of ownership between the parties. The usage and fees must be agreed upon before the sale of the sculpture. Contracts pertaining to commissioned paper sculpture models should specify the exact usage being transferred to the client. The artist must determine the specific usage and rights being transferred to the buyer and the fair market value.

For paper sculptures sold as original works of art, copyright is just as important. Photographed paper sculptures used in advertisements are often sold as original works of art. An agreement must be made by the artist and gallery or art buyer to determine the commission and selling price of the artwork. The contract should limit the reproduction usage. The artist always retains the copyright after the sale of the original work.

Although contracts can offer an artist certain protection under the law, some agreements should be avoided whenever possible. As a freelance artist, you should never sign a work-for-hire contract. Under that provision of the copyright law, the commissioned artist forfeits all copyright ownership and looses reproduction, distribution and display rights of the work. Also, the work can be re-used or altered by the buyer without compensation to the artist.

The copyright laws were established to protect the rights of the artist under the Constitution. Any infringement of these rights can be penalized under the copyright laws. For further information regarding protection of artist's rights, contact the New York based Graphic Artists Guild. The Guild was established in 1967 by professional artists concerned with industry guidelines, professional practices, ethics and fair market value for commissioned work. This organization is dedicated to fostering ethical standards between graphic artists and art buyers.

ARTIST'S DIRECTORY

Pat Allen
4510 Alpine Road
Portola Valley, CA 94028
Phone 415-851-3116
p.90-101

Johnna Bandle
J.B. Illustration
7726 Noland Road
Lenexa, KS 66216
Phone 913-962-9595 / Fax 913-962-9595
p.26-37

Cindy Berglund

Cindy Berglund Illustration & Design
5275 E. Lake Beach Court
Shoreview, MN 55126
Phone 612-490-5141 / Fax 612-490-9747
p.52-63

Marcelo Bicalho

R. Marliéria, 260
Bairro Santa Inês
Belo Horizonte -MG Brazil 31080 360
Phone 5531-486-3135 / Fax 5531-486-3135
p.114-125

Dee Deloy

8166 Jellison Street
Orlando, FL 32825
Phone 407-273-8365 / Fax 407-273-8365
p.64-75

Carol Jeanotilla

Jeanotilla Design, Inc.
120 South Fraser Circle
Aurora, CO 80012
Phone 303-360-9945 / Fax 303-360-9945
p.140-151

Joan Kritchman-Knuteson

Advertising Art Studios, Inc.
710 North Plankinton / Suite #800
Milwaukee, WI 53203-2454
Phone 414-276-6306 / Fax 414-276-7925
p.128-139

Mark Marturello

Marturello Illustration
13899 Summit Drive
Clive, IA 50325
Phone 515-226-9122
p.76-87

Koji Nakamura

A-105 City-Luck Takamatsu/2022-1 Tsuruichi-cho
Takamatsu-City, 761 Japan
Phone (0878) 82-6511 / Fax (0878) 82-9503
p.38-49

Ricardo Radosh

Ricardo Radosh - Illustrator
Presa Oviachic 178 Col. Irrigación
Mexico City, D.F. 11500 Mexico City
Phone 525-3957939 / Fax 525-3957939
p.102-113

1 **5** 5

Dimensional Illustrators, Inc.

Principals Kathleen Ziegler and Nick Greco established Dimensional Illustrators, Inc., to support 3Dimensional illustration in the advertising and publishing industries. They have produced the 3Dimensional Art Directors and Illustrators Awards Show since 1989, to recognize and honor the dimensional illustration genre and have published many books featuring contemporary illustration, graphics, design and advertising. Several books, including the *3Dimensional Illustration Awards Annual, The Best of 3Dimensional Illustration Sourcebook, Fabric Sculpture: A Step-by-Step Guide, Digitalink Digital Design and Advertising and DigitalFocus The New Media of Photography,* demonstrate their dedication to recognizing excellence in the visual communications industry.

Kathleen Ziegler is president and creative director of Dimensional Illustrators, Inc. An accomplished illustrator and lecturer, she has received numerous awards including the AGFA Achievement in Design Award. Ms. Ziegler has been featured in Step-By-Step Graphics magazine, and has recently appeared on the Lifetime TV network program, *Our Home,* to promote paper sculpture.

Nick Greco is vice president and executive editor of Dimensional Illustrators, Inc. He is responsible for overall marketing, researching and developing future publications. Mr. Greco lectures throughout the United States and abroad on artists' copyright laws and responsibilities.

Dimensional Illustrators, Inc.
362 Second Street Pike / Suite 112
Southampton, Pennsylvania 18966 USA
215.953.1415 **Telephone**
215.953.1697 **Fax**
http://www.3DimIllus.com **Website**
dimension@3DimIllus.com **Email**

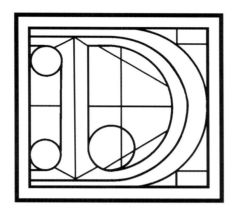

Annual 3Dimensional Art Directors and Illustrators Awards Show

The **3Dimensional Art Directors and Illustrators Awards Show** was established in 1989 by *Dimensional Illustrators, Inc.*, as an international competition to recognize excellence in 3Dimensional illustration. This unique exhibition honors paper sculptors, dimensional illustrators, modelmakers, digital and electronic artists, visual creatives and art directors.

Unlock your best work in art direction and creation of dimensional and digital illustration. Dimension as an illustrative genre demonstrates the powerful possibilities available to all visual creatives. Take this opportunity to reveal your 3D acumen in the one show dedicated to excellence in traditional and digital contemporary dimensional illustration.

Call for Entries

Categories include: magazine advertisements and editorials, brochures, books, posters, direct mail, annual reports, TV commercials, calendars, greeting cards and self-promotions.

Mediums include: paper sculpture, wood and clay sculpture, paper collage, paper pop-ups, fabric stitchery, digital & electronic media, recycled and mixed media, as well as, video animation as applied to the communications industry.

Exhibition
The 3Dimensional Art Directors and Illustrators Awards Show is exhibited annually in December at the prestigious Art Directors Club of New York.

Awards
This international show presents Best of Show, Gold, Silver and Bronze awards to 3D illustrators and art directors worldwide. Best of Show Award $1,000.

3D Awards Annual Website
Best of Show, Gold, Silver and Bronze award winners will be showcased on the 3D website: www.3DimIllus.com

Deadline
Entries are accepted year round. Annual Deadline June 30.

For a Call for Entries poster contact:
Nick Greco / Awards Show Coordinator
Dimensional Illustrators, Inc.
362 Second Street Pike / Suite 112
Southampton, Pennsylvania 18966 USA
215.953.1415 **Telephone**
215.953.1697 **Fax**
http://www.3DimIllus.com **Website**
dimension@3DimIllus.com **Email**

New Books by Dimensional Illustrators, Inc.

These publications will energize your creative endeavors and enhance your concepts. Indispensable reference guides, they feature excellence in dimensional imagery. Visual creatives, dimensional illustrators, art directors and art buyers will find these books a welcome addition to their library.

DigitalFocus *The New Media of Photography* $34.95 (includes shipping)

Experience the powerful imagery of digital photography. DigitalFocus explores the essence of both the explosive and impressive fusion of photography and digital illustration. This premiere edition applauds the diversity of this photographic genre and alters forever our perception of the camera and the computer. With more than 300 full-color examples, DigitalFocus discusses inventive software and techniques, exposing the interrelationships that exist between the origin of the idea, the creative process, and the final image. This is a vital publication for all creative visionaries seeking to explore the cyber-technology of new media photography. Chapters include: Advertising, Business, Sports, Surreal, People, Editorial and Media. *Cover image by: Nick Koudis/Cover Design & Typography by: MWdesign.*

DigitaLink *digital design and advertising* $34.95 (includes shipping)

Take a quantum leap into the electrifying age of digital design and advertising. Immerse yourself in the cutting-edge genius of computer-generated imagery. Witness the fresh, raw enthusiasm of the digital illustrator. In this showcase edition of Digitalink, you will find more than 300 captivating digital illustrations in which the ingenuity of electronic art and advertising collide. Each provocative chapter explodes with details on the software, methods and techniques that shift electronic design into high gear. This book will both inspire and excite you as you delve into the limitless potential of this new-wave media. Chapters include: Magazine and Editorial Advertising, Direct Mail, Posters, Annual Reports, Book Covers and Brochures. *Cover Design and Typography by: MWdesign.*

More Paper Sculpture: *A Step-By-Step Guide* $32.95 (includes shipping)

Expand your creative capabilities and experience a fascinating journey through the enchanting realm of paper sculpture. Ten internationally distinguished artists present all-new, hand-selected projects and gallery pieces culled from their personal portfolios. This full-color, step-by-step guide features more than 300 photographs, from layout to finished sculpture. A valuable resource for the novice or professional seeking a delightful medium for artistic expression. Stimulate your creative energies and expand your marketability in the illustration and fine art industries. This absorbing and inspirational edition reveals the technical skills used by professional paper sculptors for enjoyment, as well as, for profit. *Cover Image by: Carol Jeanotilla/Cover Design and Typography by: MWdesign.*

Contact: *Dimensional Illustrators, Inc.* • 362 Second Street Pike • Suite 112 • Southampton, PA 18966 • USA
Phone: 215-953-1415 • **Fax:** 215-953-1697 • **Email:** dimension@3DimIllus.com
For Online Orders visit our **Website:** http://www.3DimIllus.com
Method of payment: Visa, MasterCard, Check, International Money Order • International Orders add $5.00 for shipping.

3Dimensional Awards Annual Website

www.3DimIllus.com

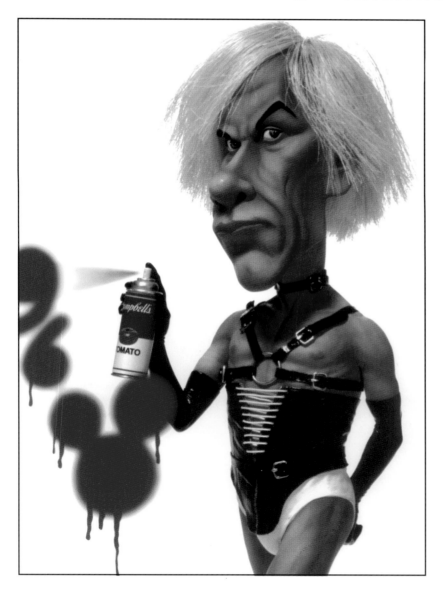

Expose yourself !

Art directors, art buyers and creative directors ...unleash the captivating power of the third dimension.

This cyber Awards Annual from the 3Dimensional Art Directors and Illustrators Awards Show showcases the Gold, Silver and Bronze winners in the form of ads, brochures, magazine covers, editorials, annual reports, calendars, books, posters, etc.

The 3D Awards Website is an international showcase dedicated to promoting and honoring the best 3Dimensional professionals in the visual communications industry.

Quickly search the 3D Awards Annual Website by Illustrator, Medium or Category to find the source for your next project.

www.3DimIllus.com

3D Illustration: **Yasutaka Taga**

Contact Dimensional Illustrators. Inc. at:

362 Second Street Pike / Suite 112 • Southampton, PA 18966 USA
Phone: 215-953-1415 • **Fax:** 215-953-1697 • **Email:** dimension@3DimIllus.com

Website: http://www.3DimIllus.com